WHEN MY SON DIED

WHEN MY SON DIED

KENN PITAWANAKWAT

WHEN MY SON DIED

Front cover illustration from painting by Jordan Quequish
Back cover photos by Allan Joyner and Karen Meawasige

Typesetting and e-book production by Chris Bell
Atthis Arts LLC, www.atthisarts.com

Editorial services by Emily Williamson
Chrysalis Editorian, www.chrysaliseditorial.com

ISBN 978-0-9949648-0-9

Visit the author at www.kennpitawanakwat.com

My life and this project could not have been possible without the unerring and continuous support from my wife Lorraine - there when I first introduced Shannon as a child. It has been love since then.

You were there Lorraine to help bring my boy home. You were there when they wheeled him out to his final resting place. And you are still there as I go through my breakdowns-never judging-ever accepting.

Miigwetch Lorraine Miigwetch, your husband who can never repay, Kenn.

To our son Dave who was there in spirit at the wake - so torn between academics and duty. Son, Shannon would not want you to fail in your studies. Miigwetch for doing so well in university. Shannon is proud of you. You made the right choice. Teresa and Ben, continue to follow your dreams. Miigwetch, Merci for making it home in one giant drive from Montreal to Serpent River in time for closing the casket.

Angie, Miigwetch for caring for me and just being there. Brian, Miigwetch for being there for my daughter. Knowing you are still there for her gives me rest and peace of mind.

Catherine and Chelsea, you are now my daughters. I need you more than you need me. Be that as it may, I will do my best to be a papa and a grandpa. Again, I wish I was there for you when you were as tiny as your dad, the day we brought him home. You are my babies. And always you shall be. Me, You, Shannon. We are one.

Karen. What can I say? No amount of words will heal. As parents, we know the indescribable pain of losing our child. I will always love you. Shannon is looking out for us. He is never far away. All we got to do is ask him to help us.

KENN PITAWANAKWAT

People to Thank

Kristopher Baron

Christopher Bell

Emily Bell

People of Birch Island First Nation

Linda Bruton

Renee Buczel

Fr. Michael David Chenier

Rita and the late Eric Corbiere

Steve Degoosh

Herta B. Feely

Marlene Finn-Wolfman

Spencer Fraley

Lloyd and Joyce Francis

Martha Gabow

Doug Gagnon

Danny Garceau

Donald Girard

Margaret Gordon

R.J. Green

Jonelle Hoffmann

Armand Jacko and family

Rachel Jacko

Gail Jacobs

Carri Johnson

Nancy Johnson

Beatrice and Martin Jones and family

People of King Fisher Lake
    First Nation

Catherine Krall Lapointe

Dr. David Luoma

Uncle Antoine Maiangowi

Donnie Maiangowi

Laura Marjory Finn and family

Joe Masters

Beatrice Meawasige and family

Bob Meawasige

Denis Meawasige and
    Claudette deVleeshschouwer

Karen Meawasige

Ken Meawasige

Kris Meawasige

Kurt and Charlotte Meawasige

Marie Meawasige

Nishin Meawasige

Shawn Meawasige

Cam and Debbie Monty

Pat Muth

Center for Native American Studies,
    Northern Michigan University

Native American Student Association,
    Northern Michigan University

Irvin Oshkabewisens

Jason Peltier

Brian Pitawanakwat

Carson Pitawanakwat

Dale Pitawanakwat and
Misty Wassegijig

Ed Pitawanakwat

Emmett Pitawanakwat

Melanie Pitawanakwat

Mildred Pitawanakwat and
Cho-Boy Shawana

Shauna Pitawanakwat

Victor Pitawanakwat

Selma Poulin

Steve and Teresa Ravenelli

Catherine Reader-Meawasige

Chelsea Reader-Meawasige

Aimee Reader-Sicoly

Barb Recollet

Sally and Eugene Recollet

Michelle Rehkopf and
Allan Joyner

Tim Richardson

Serpent River Chief and Council

Serpent River Fire Keepers

Serpent River Hand Drum Group

People of Serpent River First Nation

Brian Shawanda

Mike Shelafoe

Mike Sicoly

Sue Smart

Carol Strauss Sotiropoulos

Garnier Spanish

Nick Spanish

Hilda Tadgerson

Llyn and April Tadgerson

Kevin Timlin

Sara Jane Tomkins

David Wayne and
Charlene Pitawanakwat

People of Wikwemikong
Unceded Indian Reserve

Emily Williamson

David Wolfman

ANY OMISSIONS OR ERRORS ARE STRICTLY MINE
AND MINE ALONE—KENN PITAWANAKWAT

WHEN MY SON DIED

Dear Son: Shannon Kenneth Cecil Shantu Papase Meawasige; Thank you for opening up the heavens. Thank you for the tears and the laughter. May the wheel of life perpetuate love to our fellow beings. May kindness reach into dark and spring life and light and smiles. Much has happened since you went home.

Miigwetch for the teaching's. With each breath, each encounter with another, but most of all, the walk with the self, brings a renewed kindness and love for others. I have a ways to go.

I love you son. And I miss you so much. I have tried to show the world your spirit.

I have only one request Shantu, my son. Look after your Mom and our children.

Baa-maa-pii Ka-waab-i-min—See you later, Daddy.

Photo by Karen Meawasige, May 12, 2009—"It was at the top of 'The Midnight Dome' in Dawson City, YT. I took it because I could never have enough pictures of him."

1.

A LETTER TO YOU

As the sun rises, so shall your fire extinguish at the end of the day.
                                        —*Big Brother Nanabozho*

Dear son: I wish our story be made available to us and anyone else seeking solace from the loss of their child. Help me formulate the appropriate diction, son. I ask you to look over my shoulder and suggest ideas and memories. Give me the insight and intuition to create the appropriate message.

Since you are home in the spirit world, I call upon your spirit and the spirit of our ancestors to step in and give me a nudge here and there, so I can render a humble human touch to our memories. One day, I too will no longer be of the terrestrial. That crossing over is not far away.

Through tears I attempt to write. It's a fight. It's a struggle. For I am an angry father softened by Nishinaabe culture, language, and tradition. I seek not malice nor retribution. Peace is my only goal. Help me, son. Send me a prayer, will you not?

My wish is to help another soul in need, another father or mother to find strength in these words. The test is for me to come with the right formula. I am not strong, but I am determined to convey the power of Nishinaabe medicine, wheel, and world view. Mine is not the final answer. Mine is only one of many. But it is true. It speaks to the truth.

When you died, I died. Father and first borne. I wish our story to be public. I yearn to express the state of our lives after you died. This is my way of apologizing and confessing things I should have said and done over thirty-eight years. I want to tell about the love that kept us together. It's too late. Is it? Or, not?

You are home with our families in a remarkable community. In our home, our ancestors as medicine people keep you happy and busy. As busy as the day you travelled.

"Back to the motherland," you laugh.

Shantu, no longer are you with us my boy. My tears soak your tracks. Out of reach for the moment, I cannot wait to enter your circle of warmth.

Perhaps, we can do several things, son. I can get stuff off my chest. And perhaps, we can help someone who has lost a child. Perhaps, we can help the grieving parent, and maybe, just maybe, we can show our lives simultaneously through the Nishinaabe lens. Who knows? Maybe we can show the dynamics of modern day grief within a Native American context.

Much has been said on grief, son, but so very much less from an indigenous perspective. Maybe we can help others traverse the dead and dying road, and again, maybe, offer some inspiration and guidance. Did we not find storytelling a fun way of telling tall tales with humor? This could be a problem. As you know, I am not, presently, good with humor, son. Especially now.

To apply humor to death is unheard of or uncomfortable to most. The grim reaper topic is abhorred. Not so in Nishinaabe country. Laughter is a medicine. It's a healing medicine. One cannot go to a wake or funeral without witnessing or taking part in raucous laughter. To talk about death and dying is part of life.

Finally, we may offer suggestions of the practical sort for those bereaved. I choose to speak from a Nishinaabe father's experience. Death, especially the death of a child has become taboo with Indian country. The whole idea of dying is dismissed.

This behavior does not add to healing. The bereaved is avoided, even ignored. People that may know of one's loss suddenly lose their eyesight. They go blind. They no longer see the bereaved. Suddenly, they are transfixed on their cell phones, or something in the highway ditch. I know this because this I used to also be a part of this. I did this.

The dichotomy.

Losing you, my son, is the most devastating experience I have ever had. It's too much for any human being. I am asking you to sit with me and help with organizing my thoughts. I am at my wits end. My mind is a jumble of mash struggling to comprehend thought and writing. The two spar to not connect. Thought and mind no longer wish to partner with my fingers. The mind tells the organism it's too difficult a task and should be parked on the shelf.

Next time, it commands. It's too painful, it yells. Leave it alone. No one cares.

The keyboard ducks for cover. It seems to hide the keys. It's a burden.

Unlike you, my son, English thought and expression are a second language for me. I do not think or speak in English. I take the word or audible and send to my internal processing machine. I dismantle the word, phrase or idea. Once I have it, I then piece the expressions into Nishinaabe. Once I have ascertained that I do understand the English, through the filter of language and culture, I dig for the appropriate English response.

Meanwhile, this has taken some time. Anywhere from a second to a few minutes. Sometimes I fail to understand altogether. English is a second language for me, so I ask you to give me a hand with composition and all that goes with expression. Any errors will remain solely my own.

Nishinaabe is my way of thought and speaking. Writing, as Western culture understands, is opposite of the Nishinaabe culture. Our main communique is through art and storytelling. It's through the spoken word. Oratory is my canoe or lodge. This is my comfort zone.

I am not a great orator, as I get nervous and get tongue-tied, and in the process I lose my train of thought. Sometimes forever. So, perhaps, through the inherent cultural process of; thought diffusion and creation, I can create a workable word order, in the comfort of my space and environment, free from prying eyes. The isolated process might deliver better creative etchings.

2.

NNA-NA-BOZHO

Nanabozho wanted to communicate something. Someone whispered in his ear just as he was waking up this morning. "Tell them this," the voice went on.

"Tell them to etch a code on birch bark," the voice went on. "I will tell you exactly where and on which bark."

Nanabozho scratched his ears, rubbed his eyes, listed to one side, and let one go.

Of course, Nanabozho was not a stranger to trees, birds, mosquitos or his butt talking to him at the most inconvenient times. The language they communicated was universal. Everyone knew the other's language. It was all one.

Nanabozho took pride in his self-reliance. He was proud to create his own meals. He especially liked his homemade hamburgers he heaved and fashioned into juicy morsels. His hamburgers were the talk of the bush. He had to keep an eye on them as others took great mischief in stealing his culinary secretions. Nanabozho recalled the last time that darn buzzard landed on his marinating stool. "The rabbits on the other side of the sun need you. They are burning up. They sent me here to get you."

With a start, Nanabozho sprang into action. (A super hero would have been proud of his athleticism.) Through the cedar stand, through the poplar and birch saplings, and through the briars on the side of the hill, and up towards the white peaks, Nanabozho wasted no time.

The feet bled from the jagged rocks, the burrs stabbed, the thorn bushes just about poked out the eyes, and the skunk blasted Nanabozho with a nauseating rip that choked his throat and made his eyes drip so much he could not see, and he just about lost consciousness when he ran smack dab into a towering ankle of a man who did not even notice the insect-sized Nanabozho bounce off his moccasin. Collecting himself, Nanabozho jumped up but tripped over his crossed legs. Down he went into a knife-sharp piece of rock that looked like it was there just for him.

Undeterred, he made one more leap and was delighted to see the gleaming waters off in the north.

"Almost there," he assured himself.

Not long after his brush with the rest of the forest of trees and plant life, and assorted cousins scampering for safety, he reached the rabbit lodge, panting.

"Okay. Who is attacking you? What is going on? Where are they?" he blurted all at once.

The rabbits looked up at Nanabozho and then got a whiff of him.

"Whew! They shouted. And as quick as a hop they were out the door.

"What?!" beckoned Nanabozho. "What? Wait," he beckoned again.

"Wiinaage told me you guys were in trouble and that I should rush here and save you. And defend you," he lobbied. "So I rushed off as fast and as soon as I heard."

"What? You idiot!" Responded the bunnies, from the other side of the lodge wall. Nothing's wrong with us here. In fact, we're getting ready to tell a story about midday and how he came to have his name, Aapto-gii-zhig, they went on. "And don't come here," they shouted. "You stink!"

"Mooitch!" Nanabozho realized he had been tricked. As fast as he could he returned to his lodge beside the meadow. He was now alarmed about his meal. And for good reason, his food would have been devoured. He was so mad at himself that he tried to leap up towards the tallest crags and catch that acrimonious flock licking their beaks of any remaining morsels of Nanabozho's hamburger patties.

"I'll show them," he promised. Off in the distance he could see the buzzards lick and peck each other free of any remaining morsels as they rolled over hollering and laughing so much they almost fell off their perch. They had scored a free meal.

It was a good thing Nanabozho was a glutton. He had plenty of hamburger available for another meal. With a squat, he heaved and out came brand new mix ready for patty making.

"Satisfied, he had the final laugh, he proceeded to make big, thick, oozy, hamburgers. The etchings would have to wait until his lunch was done.

Thus the birch bark scrolls and petroglyphs from the Meso-American pyramids. These carvings and etchings were so sophisticated, no one could understand their meanings. You know why, son? Because they are not Nanabozho and of this world. Humor is not part of their composition. So they destroyed them. The darn Franciscans were the first in Meso-America. In our part of the country, it was the Jesuits, Recollets and others. But we adapted. I have adapted. Look at me, I now use the immigrant's script and language.

The immigrant language is not the one I was born and raised with. Mine was the Odawa, Pottawatomi, and Ojibwe language and culture and ceremony. This is where I speak from, son. I regret not raising you and helping you with the cultural construct that comes with Nishinaabe. It is the language and people I evolved with. Much of my words will lack the punch of the English first speaker, and this includes our people. I am actually assuming someone will read our story, son. I may lack the fluidness in reaching the Western-trained audience and by circumstance, I know without a doubt miss the indigenous, who are the focus group. So, as I write with this alien language and medium, I again ask for your input. Help me with my thoughts. Who knows, sonny? Maybe I will lose the First people and the Westerner. I do not know.

Grief is grief. In any culture. However, Nishinaabe cultural grief and its manifestations are another story. Our story will tell of the spirit, spirits, and the spiritual. Not the religious. We leave that to the theologians. Again, the spirit is universal across humanity. Whether one chooses to acknowledge it or not is of their own will. For us, we will jump back and forth between the "dead" and the "living," the visible and invisible across the Nishinaabe realm as perceived by a father and son within our tragic lens.

Virtually extinct is indigenous literature about death and dying and the spiritual Nishinaabe experience. Much exists for the mainstream. I found only one cursory academic paper online when I was scouring for help within the initial few moments, as it were, soon after the crushing news of your death tore into my soul. So desperate I was for any help, grasping at anything that might help me breathe and navigate through the conscious nightmare that took hold and has never let go, son.

It's my plan to tell my story through our experience, son. Maybe we can reach one or two individuals who may need a hand in carrying them through similar ordeals. Again, maybe they can tell their stories and help someone else. Who knows? We can try. This is not about a self-help memoir, son. Rather, it's about the ancient cultural practice of helping another. To share through stories is something we call "me-ko-waa-taag – o - zi-win." This is the non-intrusive code we live by in the Nishinaabe language, back home in Wiky.

Me-ko-waa-taag – o - zi-win is a way of jogging one's memory. Heaven knows I need this now. Many hours have I sat at an elder's side and listened. I ask one question and the answer is a story that extends into a three hour response. This is the gentle art of oral teaching in the language. Culturally, one does not tell the other what to do, rather, one tells a story, and if the listener is awake, walks away with the answer he or she sought. Sometimes. The norm is that the answer is never offered openly. Rather, it's up to the listener to sift and discern through the response. The response is never harsh, nor does it direct one either way. This is the way I raised you, son. It's the only way I know. This may explain, to some extent, why I left you to your own devices. That is, I trusted you to figure it out on your own, son. Part of this lesson, again, is taboo to command another human being. This is where free choice, free thought originated, son. Our people.

I miss you. I love you ngwis. I can't wait to join you. Until then, I choose to bare my soul, and doing so, may offer insight into my sick behaviors. Mine were dysfunctional. Absolutely. Beyond the shadow of a doubt. Yup. That was me. And it is me. And I probably showed you just how to be like me. Brilliant huh? Smart ass 'ol dad me, eh son?

At this moment, my energy is preserved for daily existence. I do not have the gumption for anything extra. My extra-curricular activity consists of lifting food to my face. I am lucky I have family preparing my meals. Most times, I am not hungry. Yet, I know, if I do not eat, I will begin to shake, and possibly roll onto the floor as my sugar drops. Most of the time I do not care. As luck would have it, or bad luck, I would drop and scare the shit out of family as they drive me to the hospital. That is the only reason I do care.

I do not want to be a further burden. I am already a burden. And then, if and when I do eat, and if I do not fall asleep where I sit, I will get the urge to straggle outdoors to the back yard and collect kindling, birch bark, tobacco, and small wood to make a fire. There I will sit for hours. Moving only to add more wood. The smell of smoke from firewood provides comfort. Here I will sit looking into the fire, lifting my head occasionally to study the clouds and their direction. I am quite happy plopped up in my worn lawn chair. I have no energy.

Some days it seems impossible to get out of bed, bathe, and function. It's a chore to wipe my ass, son. You would think a shower would be easy, but it all seems so extra strenuous. So I do go for a couple of days without bathing. By the third, I am pretty rank, and even I climb into the shower to wash my ass.

"Operation cheek detail!" as you used to holler from your shower.

I flee. I flee deep into my anatomy. Wish I could flee back into my mother's womb. I do. I do not want to be here. Protect me, Mom. Make it all go away, Mommy. I cry. Ever a big baby I feel. A grown man crying for his mommy. Ever sick. But that is the way I feel, son. Is there no one that can make all this pain and death and sadness go away?

"Is there no one who can fix this?"

My mind fights for control and to not let go. If I let go, I die. Or I will go insane. Crazy, huh, son? I fight for composure. Yet, I am scared to topple. I might topple over and pass out. I weep into a fetal position. When did I topple? I do not know how I got there. I cannot remember. The intense pain and numbness is intolerable. I want to scream. But I cannot. I seem to care for others. I do not want to scare anyone. Too much fear has already crippled the family, sonny. Fear of the known is too much. The unknown waits. And that alone scares the shit out of me. I cannot think straight. Simple tasks become monumental. Monumental effort is required. I do not have it, son.

"Shantu" I murmur.

"Shantu," again I cry. Tears race across my face.

"Shantu. I cannot speak in a complete sentence. I am unable to string a coherent thought. The malignance consumes without

regard. Each day is a replica of the other. It's so tiring. And I remain so scared. Fear fuels grief. Grief does not care if I live. Grief
has the inertia. It devours any resilience I might happen to have
son. Grief sounds too nice. Grief is a cover word for death, a rip
torn-ragged-jagged-tear-out-life sucking phenomenon that devours out from the cambium simultaneously with the maggots of
death that struck home with blunt force trauma, with the fateful
death arrow sniped with guerrilla precision. The wound hemor-
rhages life force. I have been hit. Now I labor to inhale. At times
I forget. Breathe, I say. I can see my life disintegrate into nothingness. My mind struggles to halt insanity from breaching the walls
built over a lifetime.

The palisade undergoes its first test. Nothing has ever been
so detrimental, son. Will my sanity hold? Will my body? My
body is a putrid mess of gag and vomit. Diarrhea counters with
infrequent release. My stomach churns anxiety. Hiccups reveal
hyper-vigilance. Vigilance creates panic. Panic seems to attack my
heart. More fear creeps in. How much can my heart take before it
implodes? My heart and mind race and stumble. Sometimes my
heart beats so fast and so hard, I attempt to count the minutes stolen from my original longevity. My mind jerks rampantly, outward,
backward, forward, inward with no discipline. Instead it seems to
delight itself in leading my psyche into a maze that seems point-
less and without exit. I am stuck in this churned mess.

Where do I go now? Fear grips my bladder. I urinate frequently. I counter the attack. I try for equilibrium. I fear I will lose.
Someone please, make it all go away.

My mind screams silently. Help me! But no one hears. And
the sad part? No one can say or do anything that can help.

Flashes of good times and good feelings race across. But my
mouth cannot smile. My mind sees only a dark apocalypse. I do recall the warm feeling of love. The warmth disappears, devoured by
paralyzing dread. My base pulsates. Intense rigor fights for control.
Domination keeps me immobile.

Anything productive that may have once kept me going and
going about my way through the day has vanished. I do recall off
and on that I used to be a contributing member of my family and
community. I used to be a beacon of measured response. This was

back when I embraced and welcomed the day's trials, accomplishments to be had, and giving thanks for lessons learned before I retired each day.

The only accomplishment that I cherish and hold on to now with all my strength is knowing that you are okay and in the hands of safety and love. Your final destination has been reached.

Your final resting place is now home. You are not left to wander between worlds. To know you glow in another realm and are able to traverse back and forth to this plane is good enough for me. You are free! No more pain for my boy, Shantu, is good enough. Leave me to concentrate on one breath at a time. Where this life takes me is irrelevant.

Thank you for your last visit. It has been a great comfort to me to know you are still with us each day. I miss your laugh, jokes, and zany one-liners, son. Wish I could replace those thirty-eight years.

Shantu. Shantu. Hear me, son.

3.

NNGII-BII-DAA-JIM
(THE FORETELLING)

I remember the time you told me about the locator gadget you wore skiing. Of course I had no idea what that was. With great relish, you told me it was for finding buried bodies under the snow. Braving the avalanche-prone areas in the outback was of great excitement for you. I, of course, was shocked to understand the gravity of your escapades. And no amount of cajoling could change your mind. Not that I tried too hard. But I think you knew your pops was not too happy about this revelation. You smiled, son.

Clunk! Clunkety clunk. That was the sound of your head as it met with the precipices hidden under the powder. Did you learn? Of course not. My boy, that scared some of the crap into tight little hamburgers. These lil' chunks of poo are now the ones that slip out as reminders of our banter. I now look back at these antics as the qualities that made my boy. You were one of a kind, son. Memories keep me going. Shantu, my boy, guide my thoughts and words with light, grit, and power. My son, I had no idea I was so happy until you died.

It's been a year since you went to join Grandma, Grandpa and so many other family members. Our blood is of medicine. This is our medicine circle. And I am proud to have shared some of our traditions, sonny. Wish I could have done more. I know it's irrelevant now.

It was beautiful to participate in ceremony. Ancient, ancient ways that you are now a part of, with ancient, ancient ancestors, men of power, skill, and knowledge. More than I will ever know. The circle of medicine men healing the bereaved—the ones left with inconsolable pain. My heart rises with joy as I know you stand with the old ones. You heal with them as an equal. My god! The power of creation. Where we come from and to the place we return. You earned it, son. You deserve every inch of the happy and all-powerful knowledge, son. Miigwetch for looking after your poor old pops and the rest of us left behind in shreds. On their behalf, I say thank you. I know many of them are not privy to your place and stature. But they would be happy to know that you are happy and stand with the great ones. Men so old, and of another time, that none of us knew who they were. But, there you were. One of them! Singing and praying in unison with those ceremonial rattles that the sacred group each held and shook the world. I want to be with you.

Miigwetch for bringing the sacred hoop, son. It's a start. From here I have begun to heal. It's funny how we came to notice it. One morning, we noticed your friend the bunny rabbit sitting adjacent to the rear of the shed in the backyard. Why that spot, son? If it marks the spot for ceremony, it's located in a kinda awkward place. Anyhow, we watched the brown bunny sitting there, all cool and everything. He or she sat there cool like I said. And he was not moving. He was stationary. Odd, as those lil' guys will munch away and maybe inch this way or another. This went on some fifteen minutes or so. But it was long enough to bring a smile. Thought nothing of it other than it was a bunny. Or, was it? Maybe it was you. Maybe it was Nanabozho.

I was asking myself, is that Nanabozho? Because we know that dude can change himself into any form. Well, we left the critter to itself and went about our business. I then got the bright idea to go out to the spot where waabozo sat and investigate. I was quite surprised, son. Where he sat was an almost perfect circle of dark green grass that stood out from the regular growth of weeds we accept as lawn. And which I keep mowing every week or couple of weeks, depending on its height. Or if it's green and not brown from sunstroke or lack of rain.

I stood outside the circle. I took in as much as I could absorb. Okay. From what I could observe, the bunny sat inside the now visible circle. He sat smack dab in the middle inside the hoop. Never have I witnessed a dark green anything circle in my yard. Ever. I have seen circular lodgings and other assorted frames. But this was something new. Even exciting. And just like a real Indian, I must have grunted something like, "Hmm."

I surmised the mark to be about three feet in diameter. The edge of the hoop about four to five inches in width.

"Okay, Bunny, what are you trying to tell me?" I thought.

I knew it was something so I went back indoors and got my semaa. I walked back and made a tour around the circle clockwise. I do not know when or where I picked up this practice, son, but I circled clockwise, outside of the circle perimeter. I then returned to the spot where I previously stood facing west. I took the tobacco out from the pouch with my right hand. I then sprinkled it on top of the perimeter clockwise. I again made a complete circle. For each quadrant I said the name. I began at my feet then worked south.

"Zhaawanong. Epinigizhimowok. Giiwedinong. Waabanong."

I finished with a miigwetch.

Satisfied that I had delivered the proper respect and thanks-giving, I took a few more minutes with my inspection, circled maybe one more time, then walked back indoors.

Sometime after, I had my cousin who is an herbalist unex-pectedly drop in. He was coming from the bush in South Bay and was stopping by to visit. Good thing I was home.

"Kaawiin. Nope. I have never seen anything like it either," he shook his noggin.

His inspection also included the full circuit. He asked if I had seen the doorway opening on the north side. "Holy crap," or something like that, I must have said. As out-of-it as I was, I must have missed it on the first tour. He, being of sound mind and body, noticed it right away. I bent over closer to the opening which now appeared clearer. Sure enough, the circle dropped off at the open-ing. And this was the direction the bunny had been facing. North. I told him so. But, what I did notice was a particular mushroom that now grew within the dark green outgrowth itself. Not inside the hoop. Not out. Not anywhere else. But all through the budding diameter. We looked at each other, and he too sprinkled his semaa on the outcrop.

"Nanabozho naa?" I said.

He nodded. "Indeed, this is something," he agreed in Nish.

I was referring to the bunny. I was convinced the bunny was Nanabozho. He had come to visit and bring strength for which I was in dire need, son. Were you aware of this appearance, son? Or was that you?

My cousin and I agreed to keep mindful of the hoop. Through

the summer and up until I had to leave the rez for work back in the States, that circle has been there along with its crop. Since then I have entered and left the circle from the northern doorway opening. Each time I feed the enclosure and hoop with semaa and a thanksgiving. Will we meet inside there sometime, son? Or is that a replica of the hoop you now reside in? Is it my hoop to enter and seek healing?

I have sat in there a couple of times. It's a good thing my yard is enclosed by an eight foot high slat fence, son, or folks might just think crazy of me. Maybe I am. Maybe it's all a joke.

Something to make me laugh. Sometime. Not now. At best, I can produce a smile. With no sound.

It's a wonder I never took the time to show you the full wonders of Nanabozho. My fault. But you know all, son. So I do not feel that bad about it in those terms. But I failed to provide while you were on this earth. Nanabozho came to teach your cousin.

One time he was dancing like no one had seen before. When asked who had taught him to dance like that, he responded, "Nanabozho."

His dad still talks about that. And your little cousin was only four or five at that time. And no way could he pick moves up like that anywhere in Pow-Wow country. They remain secret to this day. His Dad and I talked about that recently. The wonders of the Indian world. Locked away. Not meant for public display.

So who brought who? I do not know. Nor does it matter. Either way, you were there. And that bunny rabbit Nanabozho has not returned. So I wish to thank you and Nanabozho. Miigwetch for your strength. Miigwetch for your fortitude. Miigwetch for giving me something to look forward to. And inward. And all around.

This medicine wheel is a first for our home, son. This wheel of life sustains me. It keeps me from dying of grief, son. I miss you.

I thank our maker for bringing us together, son. I thank the creator for the gift of healing and language, respect and use of the sacred pipe, tobacco, and the hoop of tradition. The bond continues. There might have been division, son, but love kicks ass. Light perseveres. Our lives, however brief, are led by Gizhe-manido, the kind maker of light and dark, the positive and not so positive. Nanabozho, his lieutenant, continues to teach. I am so sorry for my neglect. I apologize for not teaching the nuts and bolts of our language. No matter, eh, dude? You now know the secrets of the universe.

The roles have changed. I now take lessons from you. Willingly I follow. I discern and try to change my behaviors. It's a battle. An internal struggle. It does not help that I am in an extreme state of loss. But somehow, I find myself here. You are my Nanabozho, son. You are my teacher. My guide. Strength. And solace. Source of much memory. The good. The reality that reminds me that a simpleton is all we are comprised of. And in the end, ashes, dust, fodder for the grass, fungi and creatures.

For this I am grateful. Forever, ever so grateful. Every day, son. And I cry.

I try to savor the memorable moments of our lives, son. Much escapes me. The scary part is that our moments may have been erased. Pray this is not so. Help me remember the good and simple memories that we shared.

I suppose I want to begin with the first days. The sunrises that made our moments. There are many I do not recall. Some show up. One of the early images is the cone head memory. Your head was really in the shape of a cone when you emerged into this world. An alien. Yikes!

You came as a scary critter. Wasn't funny then, but now it reveals the nature of your funny bone. But I still loved you. You made us laugh, son. You made us feel good while you were here.

Remember the time you saw one of the street names in Wiky –Amikook, and without missing a beat you said, "I'm a kook."

Did we not snort in laughter that time?

My tears seem to have swept my memory. I cannot remember much. I'm surprised when I am told Shannon said this, did this, or that. Yet I was there. I am told so. Maybe, some time, my memory will return. In the meantime, I will stick to those moments my internal hard drive has retained. Sometimes I remember after the fact. Someone tells a story, then I remember. I guess those memories are in there someplace. Just have to dig them out, son.

As I look back, these brief moments prepared me for your leaving early. I was blissfully unaware. I am not sure just exactly how they prepared me. Someone has to explain it to me.

It's something I sense. I cannot come up with the words. My brain is fried. But my body and spirit tell me there is more. Such is the blow of your death. In some ways it left me crippled. I yearn for answers. Answers are slow to appear. Maybe I am in too much of a rush. What is that? Is it even this? Possibly I am barking up the wrong proverbial tree.

It is like holding back the child from harm. As a parent, my job has always been to protect you. I slog through each day looking for something that will make sense of this insanity. One of those ways is research. I ask questions.

I was talking to my good friend Nick who also lost his son recently. Have you met his son? Is that how it works? Or not? Again I was not there for Nicholas, save for maybe a phone call. I had no idea the crushing weight he was going through at the time. It was all so very tragic. Being an idiot, I went to visit him. Nick and I played together as kids. We grew up together. He too came from a large family. Later on we both came to work together professionally across health centers in Ontario. He was a trained Counsellor. But after the death of his son, he too, from what I could see from a distance, was no longer employed. I could not appreciate the destruction of his world. It was only after you left that our lives again connected in a manner no one should encounter. So I went to visit him looking for answers. He was kind enough to welcome me with open arms and candor. This was the one brief interlude with an authority. One who knows the death of a child. Unless one knows this darkness, one has no idea what they are talking about. I know this.

I was looking for some insight. At the same time, because of our zany, internal shared experiences from working and growing up together, I also was looking for some brief release through fun stories. It was all in the language. He is also fluent in Nishinaabe and not as well spoken in English as I am.

He's a character. Just like all of us. He's darker than me and his hair is white like mine. His smile is punctuated by pearly white teeth, which actually shows off his skin color. And he is an inch or two taller. And he is thinner. I now am the pudgy one. He laughs at that sometimes. Makes fun of me. It makes me laugh. He knows he can get away with it. And he is not shy to deliver funny anecdotes. Many are exaggerated. Most are at my expense. So, he's a safe source of confidence.

We were sitting in his apartment. He laughed at me when I told him that I wake myself up with restless leg syndrome and how irritating it is, especially when one is going through a very painful episode and not getting enough sleep.

"You remind me of the dog," he grinned. "If you watch the dog," he continued between guffaws, "the dog will shake himself awake."

With a holler and back toss of his brown and white noggin he immediately set the bar for our meeting. We had not seen one another for a couple of years. He was in Sudbury and I was away in the States.

"If you pay attention to the dogs, they shake themselves awake. Perhaps they were dreaming. Maybe they are dreaming about the meal lost to another dog," he continued. He inhaled the smoke from his cigarette and waited for my response. Seeing there was none, his grin punctuated the fact that he had more to say.

I was lying flat on my back on the floor. This is now my routine position, as I am too drained to even sit up. Plus, I was tired from driving some two hours from the rez.

"What they dream about we do not know. Or, maybe . . ." He paused to sip at his coffee, something he likes to do any hour of the day. I cannot. Normally, coffee is off limits after mid-afternoon, as it will keep me awake all night long. Not pleasant. Today was an exception. I was having one with him as I could not tell if it was late, early, or whatever. I also did not care, as I was not sleeping anyway. Plus, I did need the coffee for the three hour return trip back home.

He continued with his wisdom. I say that with Indian humor. Meant to be laughed at, yet lessons were in there somewhere. With emphasis, he said, "They will stop to bite at their scrotum trying to catch that elusive tick that's making a meal chomping their balls. He'll stop only after he is satisfied that he ate the critter. Then he will lick his balls. Maybe that is what you should do," he grinned.

I may have grinned like a foolish Indian at that point. Indian jokes abound, eh, son?

He stopped to gaze out the window only a cheap apartment

will flaunt. He lit a second smoke and blew forward his first smoke signal.

"Enhh . . ." he nodded, indicating he was not done.

He was still smiling, although not as wide. But it was still there. Occasionally, and for very few bursts in between, I saw the pain of his loss shoot across his face and just as quickly disappear. His usual grin, barely noticeable, returned ever so slightly. He sat there in his sagging sofa chair. I was splayed out on the floor as I had not the stamina to sit up. I had also spilled my coffee on the floor. With an exaggerated groan he slowly pushed himself off his chair and walked to kitchen, all the while groaning,

"Gegowa gegoo nendige," playing clown and old man.

Well, he was an old man, was he not? It used to be a running joke between us before we turned fifty. We enjoyed needling the other with reminders, hey! Almost fifty years old now, eh? It was a way to laugh. This was before we both lost our hearts.

Shuffling back from the kitchen, he groaned as he stooped down to one knee to clean up my mess. "Perhaps, I'm a dog also," he added. "Here I am licking the old man's stuff," he ribbed. Satisfied the coffee had disappeared from the floor, he returned the stained dish cloth to the kitchen, and ever so slowly it seemed, walked back to his chair and dropped his behind in it.

He is a character. Everything is laborious. He gripes about his aches and pains and "arthur-itis" as he calls it. I've learned to let his griping go in one ear and out the other.

"Do not make me get up again," he said, admonishing me, as if it took a herculean effort to get up from his worn crusted chair I know has seen better days, go the kitchen, look for a very stained face cloth that served as a dish cloth, drop to the floor, rise to return the article, and head back to his perch. I ignored him.

His role playing games as a decrepit old dog continued. Like any old dog, his antics served to exaggerate his arthritis and waning years. Hell. I know dogs that can move faster than that. And I relished telling him so. He always laughed. We would go back and forth with our admonishing, then continue after we caught our breath. At this time, the old dog as I would have called him had I not been so drained, too tired to even return fire, was pretending to be greatly inconvenienced. He was studying me. As I him. We only looked at one another when we had to have the other repeat what one had just said. Otherwise, we knew where the other was by the inflection and tone of the voice. He was waiting to see my reaction. I had not said a word. Satisfied I was not going to run away from his insults, and our game was still in play, he extinguished his smoke. We were now in a cloud of smoke.

The smell of tobacco is either a comfort or a revulsion for me, son. Today, whatever it was, did not matter. His place. He could do whatever he wanted. I had to have one and groped for my jacket, found my smokes, and offered the smoke to the sky.

"Ever good you," he replied.

A pause of silence followed. He sat in his perch and I was still horizontal on the floor. We breathed in each other's second hand smoke. In my case, I was offering you a smoke, son. I guess my friend had maybe forgotten to do his offering for the day, or he was glad to see me communicate with the great unknown, or whatever. No matter.

"Yup. We are like old dogs." He added.

Now he was including himself in the story. I pounced, "Sometimes I scratch myself awake."

"Ge-debiwe-ton gwo!" he shot back with a choking cough.

One can only imagine the scenarios playing out in his lil' brain as he prepared himself with just the right type of counter.

It is true. Sometimes. Most times. I do scratch myself awake. I was curious to see if he was continuing his dog imagery. And I had joined the storytelling to goad him.

"Now, listen to what you are saying. You are wrecking my story," he exaggerated.

Undeterred, Saint Nick went on and prodded. "Show me how that's done. You must look funny nibbling your balls," he laughed out loud. Then he paused, "If only I had the ability to raise my leg that high."

"Get the brown lady to teach you how," I shot back.

"Naaaaahh," he volleyed, almost dropping his cigarette. He hollered with laughter. He knew exactly what I was saying. With his grin of white and brown, his denial was accentuated with high cheek bones, "She is your girlfriend."

The brown lady was a consistent player in our raggin' over the years. This is my version.

"You still going out with her?!" I said, mimicking the annoyance, masking the disgust someone had leveled at St. Nick some years back. She always occupied a special place in our play ever since she had unceremoniously dumped Nicholai, another name I have developed for him, and lifting his one and only department credit card as she left the building one eventful morning. This was immediately after she had planted a wet slop of a kiss on him as he left for work. The echo bounced off the bare apartment as he called for her at the end of the day. Hehe. Still funny to this day, sonny.

"Nahhhh, that's what she did to you," he was quick to return. It was as if a quick retort would somehow distance her and her bittersweet actions. Poor Nick.

"You should give her a call. I heard she was looking for you," he attacked again.

I laughed. I think it was at this one time that I actually laughed, son. Satisfied we had beaten the brown lady story to death, a quiet settled in the room. Nicolai gazed out and beyond the cracked window. I laid on the worn parquet floor, studied the intricate brown stains of whatever was on the gypsum ceiling. The ceiling might have been eggshell-colored in its day.

From an eternity of trust earned through childhood play and whispered understandings, and now, the shared pain of death, Nick continued. The ribbing seemed to end for the moment. He lit another smoke and blew a fart for emphasis.

"Careful, you're gonna blow us up," I complained. "You should scrape your underwear."

He laughed.

"Yes. Little boy," he continued to ignore my protest. "Or," he exhaled. Still smiling. He continued, "He may open an eye." He had returned to the dog story. "Not fully." He went on to describe how the mutt may just lay there and flex his muscles, stretch, yawn, and turn over and just as quickly go back to sleep and presumably dream. If dogs dream.

"Soon enough, the dog will jerk from his slumber and yelp." His words took on more of a serious tone.

"I don't know why he may shake wake himself awake," I said,

trying to sound like a wise man with much more to tell. I was told to be patient.

Not fooling anyone, my Nanabozho continued.

"Or, he will kick his legs out as if he was running away from something, and wake himself up," continued my elder. Was he telling me something, this sage, this wise old rez dog of an elder? And just as quickly, "That is what you remind me of," the old one yapped.

That was the last time I saw St Nicholai. He filled a void that time – if only for a moment. But it was something. Albeit, it was all too brief. I suppose that is why I enjoyed the comradery with Nick, my son. I know I can say anything to him. My words may sting. But that is okay. I know he can take it.

I now know his pain.

He took the time to share a story.

"I know what it feels like," he told me over the cell when I first called him. Sometime during our visit, he said with clear conviction, "Mowin. Cry. Cry any time you want. Anytime, anywhere. Because I still do," Nick confided.

I have.

This was the reason I sought him out, son. I knew he knew. He would know the devastation I was going through. This, a lifetime of play and now a bond created by one of the most unimaginable horrors.

He holds a special place. His membership in the club of parents who have lost children outdates mine. The dead lodge membership. So he is my elder. He is one I can confide in with total candor. Anytime. Is this not a gift, son?

The loss of our children. Oh, the pain of it all. Yet, we get up each day. We crawl up full height, or at least try, to meet the unrelenting cycle of sleep, no sleep, sleep again, no sleep again, and yet carve a smiley for the rest of the world. Oh, the drain of it all. I wish it wasn't so, son.

Give me strength, my boy. Do not ever stop helping your old man, your Pops, your

"Pater."

He grows old, tired, beaten, dried, and shriveled. I need all the help I can get, son. Help me.

I crave unpain. Is that a word, sonny? Who cares, eh? I ache for the going-about-my-business-and-remain-clueless-about-losing-my-child feelings.

Much life and death has touched me since your passing, son. Over twelve full moons we have had stars extinguished. Have you met them? Do you meet them when they arrive? What do you say to them? What do they say? What is their reaction to their new home? My comprehension is nil.

I only have seen the occasional flash into this world.

There were times it kicked the shit out of me. I know it has the power of lightning. I know because I have touched it, or rather, it has touched me over the years. A puny human cannot remain standing or alive after such an experience, son. Not I. A touch is more than enough. A glancing blow will suffice. I know this is your world now, son. And for that, and to know you are in good hands is enough.

"My job here is done." Remember that son?

Remember you used to say that when you had completed the dish detail or when "operation scrub cheek" had been accomplishd? Always made me laugh.

4.

GAA-BI-JI-GIING
(From Seed)

*"I know things were strained last time some . . . my fault
. . . as well . . . just me in my ways some time . . ."*

Remember this last email son? These last words I cherish.
The actual script location on my computer remains lost. I
cannot remember when we had our last actual conversation over the phone or in-person.

"Yeah, sure Dad." I hear.

I think the original email is buried deep in my archives, or
I fear it might have been erased in one of my back-up sessions.
Nevertheless, I am glad I have it. It tells a lot about our last few
months. We were estranged there for a while. Why, son? Perhaps
a look back on my twisted life may explain my shortcomings during these last moments. And perhaps this examination can explain
how I came into this world damaged. This wreck of a human being
that you called "Dad, Pater, old man," and more, may illustrate our
relationship.

Perhaps, eh? ". . . Your ways . . ."

Your ways were my ways, son. I made you that way. For this
failure on my part, I take full responsibility. I deeply regret. You
were my love, and I will love you as long as I am conscious. I
love you. And I miss you so much. Words that are unable to fully
describe this expression of my love through wandering animations
may at least manage to explain my undying love, sonny.

The last endearing email from you, is a good starting point as
any to describe our joy and trials. Without you, joy cannot exist. I
would not be sitting here trying to come up with the right words
to describe our story, or at least mine. I know you are looking over
my shoulder. Do not stop. If nothing else, I will have at least tried
to reconcile my faults. So, this my story. The story tells of where my
failings might have originated. This story is real.

I never have lost a child. I have not gone through anything

23

remotely close. Maybe I'll complete the story before I join you. Maybe, just maybe, others will read it and make sense of your dad and subsequently you and your life. Who knows? Who knows if anyone will care?

∽

The heart-piercing strike of death that came with the phone call. The phone call message that forever changed my life and killed me. I do know I will never be the same. I know. I know we are told never to say never. But that is the way I feel now, sonny. Forever I am a changed man.

"What does not kill you makes you stronger" is an empty platitude. Bullshit, I say. Define stronger. "God never gives you more than you can handle" sounds so hollow. Who came up with these bullshit ideas, son?

Ba! Humbug, eh, son? Your leaving knocked the shit out of me, and killed me in so many ways. I am still sorting it out. The assault was incapacitating. The strike on Pater and to my very soul, mind, body, left a hemorrhaging hemorrhoid of a wreck that fumbles through darkness. The way out, or in, up or down, yes or no, remains a major effort. A simple chore takes minutes to decipher. For instance, the menu.

"Come on, Kenn, she's only asking what you want to drink." Such was one encounter at a restaurant when I could not decide between a coffee, water, or soda. Everyone laughed.

Recluse should now be my name. I withdraw and tremble at the sheer demands of life. I do not answer the door, the phone, or seek conversation. I do not have the gumption, sonny. Nor do I care. I care not for what folks think of me. I live in my cocoon. Alone. Morph into what? It remains to be seen. I may never come out of my hole. And the hell with those who think whatever of me. I do not care.

∽

I know I am not the first to lose a child, nor will I be the last. But somehow, I feel, my journey with Shannon Kenneth Cecil Meawasige, Shantu, my boy, was unique. You were my first born son.

I ask your spirit to point me towards the light. I have frequently offered tobacco, food, drink, and prayer. I have used my mind and words in my frequent requests. I continue to ask for spiritual, emotional, physical, and mental strength for healing. I also ask that you guide me with the necessary ideas, words, and diction. I want to uncover my weaknesses. And being such a mess, I do so need much guidance. I cannot do it alone. Much I will tell, much I will retain.

Your guidance is vital. Help me explore and disclose my dysfunction and how it disfigured your life. It may shed some light on otherwise seemingly acceptable behaviors. I loved you so much, son, but there was something that led us to distance ourselves from the other. What was that? On my part, it's as if there was a part of me that was distant, yet warm from my heart to you. I allowed this gap to widen. What made me into such a judgmental father?

I have often said that I would've been a good soldier and would have signed up when I was of age. But I did not know about the armed forces on the rez, or in high school. I have said I would have been a good soldier because I would not have felt anything. I could take a life. Back then. Looking back, I probably would've come back with PTSD – if I returned. I imagined myself a Special Forces type of guy.

So there was a part of me that grew into whatever monster I developed into. Questions remain. How and where did I come to be this way?

I regret that cold detachment, which is my way of explaining myself when we withdrew from each other for a few months. It could not have been more than a year. Was it? Tell me I wasn't that stupid. So what made me wait for you to make the first move? I assume this is what I did. Tell me I was not that immature.

And here you are saying, it was just my way. Son. I take full fault for this. It was my direction. It was on my cue and direction, although probably unknown to you at the time, that you blame yourself.

I created you. The mini me. At the same time, I know and want you to know you were not the cold, detached immature, grotesque creature I was. And am.

At the same time, I hear you. And I love you even more for taking responsibility, real or not. That is the one good thing I like to think I gave you. Maybe not. But I do remember or sense that there was a part of me pulling towards accountability and taking responsibility. In several ways, I know the hypocrite I was. Probably still more so. But I have been trying to change over the years. It took that crash dive I had a ringside seat to some time ago when PTSD reared its ugly head.

The cross roads in that email and the eventually final, final, separation at your passing has caused heart-wrenching self-examination. Made more difficult as it's kinda hard to look at myself through tears. I am left alone to blame myself for all the short comings I've tarnished your soul with. No problem. I blamed myself for everything. I have no problem with it.

The final fork in the trail son. Looking back at that juncture, it's too late to say what I should've said and done with you, my love. Now here we are. You are in one place and I in the other. I cannot access your world as easily as I could have on this plane by picking up the phone. I am relieved and look forward to your occasional visits. To know this brings some therapy. But I still cry at the drop of hat.

Your journey's end is the best. Mine? I am not there. Yet. My path is full of sink holes. The only thing that keeps me on track, son, is that I do not have the energy to seek alternate venues. Maybe I do not want the assistance. Who knows? Probably not. All I know is I have to keep on track. Where it leads, no one can tell. I am so close to saying the hell with it all.

Maybe that is why I feed you a lot. As I do I know you have to eat also, although, you are spared the physical trial of trying to munch steak toothless. But as I told you, spirits eat through the smoke, or the spiritual. I was happy to leave your birthday dish on the granite ledge for the wind and creatures to eat on your behalf. You might have come as a winged creature. Who knows? This is also the reason why I also feed my spirits. Even though I know they are present twenty-four-seven, it's so tempting at times to resign, and forget about them. And me. Nice role model, eh, son? Just beautiful.

"It's what the French call grim." Hahaha.

You used to make me laugh with that exclamation. I can hear you now. Laughing at Pops. It's okay, son. I got to get it out. Release is good. Yeah, grim, is probably a good word to set the tone. Like I said, this is my story told within our collective experience. It's a broad sweep, I know.

But we are Indian, or Injuns, as they call us. And it is our world, The Aboriginal. This is the life we were born into and grew up in. Me and you. The world of dreams, visions, spirits, and the brutal reality of life and death from the first day of our lives. If we made it this far.

Born Indian today as it was yesterday is a daily battle with the status quo and our own people. The language, culture, and song and the great powers that kept us alive for millennia has not totally gone the way of dodo. We retain the living proof. Maybe we can draw others to come out of their lodges and share their stories. We as a people have a lot to share. Our story offers a brief glimpse of other worlds and how we interact with them on a regular basis and they are both a part and the whole of our existence. We personify our grandfathers', grandmothers' sage practices. This is the skill and art and knowledge and the power of our medicine, self-care, and healing. As our ancients before us, maybe we can offer some solace or suggest some awareness to those who have undergone life-changing, horrific events and disbelief.

I have found listening or being attached to someone who has gone through an addiction or other trauma is the best source for help. Someone who has gone through the same experience. The theoretical, book-learned idiot cannot offer tangible or first-hand understanding. Let's help the paralyzed. Those stuck in a quagmire. First-hand accounts remain unparalleled.

I aged ninety-eight years when you died. Might as well be ninety-eight years of oldness, the way I feel. Oldness? Is that a word, son? No matter. Who cares!

I had no idea. No idea you were going to die, son. Yet, the signs were there. The woodpecker's ominous knocking on my entry post would come to reverberate in my mind. I was just too dumb to notice. Had I known your name, I would have known something dark was on the horizon. But more about that later.

I fought back. I writhed. That's all I had. I fought to breathe. Many times I forgot to breathe. True. Choking soon followed. The choking was violent. The choking was violent enough to dangle me at the precipice between death and life. The edge of what? My death? My final breath? I yanked on the oxygen as hard as I could. For a long moment, I knew I was not breathing. Not taking in any air. I was immobile.

My attempt to regain breathing triggered the fear factor. I got scared. Immediately. Yet I knew in my mind that I was not afraid to die. Yet, here I was terrified. What is that, son? On the one hand I was unafraid of dying, anytime, anywhere, and yet the body went into shit mode and was fighting to grasp life. Is that the autonomic response they describe?

If so, I know what it feels like. Mentally, emotionally, and every which way, I had long ago fashioned this belief and acceptance and inevitably of death, and was quite accepting of its arrival. Yet, here I was, gripped by fear of dying?

Choking and gasping for air is not a new sensation. It was something I experienced years ago when sleep apnea arrived and literally took my breath away. My throat was constricted, causing me to stop breathing many times a night or anytime I had a nap. It was only after a decade or so I was diagnosed through sleep lab and issued a CPAP machine immediately, as the doctor and technicians discovered I had quit breathing some two hundred times in one short night. I was the most severe case they'd ever encountered. So, yes, I did know about the choking and terror.

I had dismissed this phenomenon as normal. Did everyone not go through this? I had no idea sleep apnea was a condition that existed and could lead to organ failure and even death because the body was not getting enough oxygen. Silly me, eh, son?

Looking back, I must have been a walking zombie Indian, son. I knew that would make you laugh.

All this time when I was driving in the city, rez, and highway miles, and with passengers, I was taking many lives into my own hands. Scary. I remember pulling the car over many times on the highway and having a quick nap. Five or ten or fifteen minutes was all I needed. I knew this because the choking would wake me up and off I went again until the next nap. Many times I would drive with my eyes closed while maintaining a strong will not to fall asleep. Having passengers in the car usually helped to keep me alert and not have to close my eyes. Driving alone, I was more confident I could get away with it. I always made sure oncoming traffic was nil.

The proof is the deep-set circles under my eyes. I look like a sick, old, rabid raccoon.

Agony does not take a break. I am in dead agony, twenty-four-seven. I cannot breathe. Agony does not take a break. Ever. Agony is death's friend, ally, and partner. The agony sucks the life out of me, son. Any life I may have once lived has been eliminated. It's gone. Any light that may have once clothed frolic and laughter has been extinguished.

Torture has replaced levity with a bone-crushing weight on my person. Torture arrived as a dead weight that made itself at home on my sternum. Why there? From there, this combo of pain, this life-sucking agony has radiated out to all quadrants of my psyche.

This combination's only mission is to seek and destroy. Nothing else. The onslaught has been successful. The breastplate can only take so much. How long will this last, son? How long will I last? How long can I exist in dead numbness? My existence is crushed. Mincemeat is now my name. Chopped, quartered, diced, and minced, into a sick and empty revolting carcass.

Daily existence began as war. My task was to immediately lose or push off or pull off this creature that was intent on taking my life. It has not been going well.

The fight to wrestle free from this creature was new. It was a demon I'd never encountered. I am sure it came from the nether-worlds. It's left me to shake, tremble, forget, hyper-ventilate, and not care if I live. Yet, I found myself mimicking the motions to live. That was a classic. At least to me, it was, son. I did not welcome any of its legion of mercenaries.

By the way, have I told you lately, I love you and I miss you so much? Just checking, my son.

The dead lodge membership does not offer a cradle to rest. It does not offer a time out. No breaks for the wicked. No place to lie in repose, son. I need sleep. And the rest that comes with undisturbed sleep. I am so tired. I am so tired of being tired. I ache to break free from loneliness. Sleep seems to be my only shelter. It seems to be my only break from the sorrow. Or I can start drinking.

I remain a hollow Indian. Any reserve I may have accumulated leaks away from every nook and cranny.

Tomorrow is unwanted, for it brings more fatigue, strain and pain. I am over loaded with grief. Add dazed and traumatized and numbed. The trauma smothers as it numbs. Why do I fixate on numb, son? Because, it is the only way of describing a shit kicking brutality unleashed on a humbled and previously, and seemingly, bliss existence. I would have preferred to not know this pain, sonny. Pain and numb are a pair. They are a pair of killers.

One does not live or exist without the other. Numbness makes my entire body prickle. Prickle is a prick, son. Prickle is a nauseating, numbed ass'ole of a feeling. Prickled feet, arms, legs, fingers keep me nauseated with a never ending loop of numb, and the urge to throw up. Meanwhile, I cannot move. I am paralyzed in and out. I slump in exhaustion.

I am moored like a turtle on its back. I kick and stretch trying to break free. My shell keeps me weighed down in some dead land terrain. I can only reach to offset myself. Upset from death's grip I locate myself laying horizontal on the floor, couch, bed, or the ground where I must have dropped some time ago. I am a lifeless worm of nothingness. It may take hours to move from this spot. I am paralyzed. I remain stuck. I am glued like a fly to a web.

My mind and body refuse to collaborate. Anytime day or night, day in day out, is of no consequence. I remain there in darkness. Sometimes when the sun is coming up, I may drop into sleep or wake to another nightmare. Frustrating how the darkest part of the night seems to bring repose or nightmare, son. I swear I will go insane. Maybe that will be the escape I seek. And maybe I welcome it. Maybe this cusp is the only good thing in my life.

Now that I am an active fellow in the exclusive, members-only club of parents who have lost their lives through the death of their children, I can go forward to remind myself to cherish life. Sometimes, and very briefly, and yet so deep, I feel it so. Membership is expensive. Very expensive. The entry fee requires the death of your child. Holy shit! I did not ask to join this club.

"Why Me, Lord?" Kris Kristofferson sings.

May no one else join. It's not that I invite exclusiveness, or pretend to be uppity. Hardly. I wish I had never heard of it, sonny. This lodge for the dead is a sad commentary on life and living, son, if one wants to call it living. The death of a child is only the beginning of a sad trudge through a tear-stained existence. Bitter thoughts held in check do not seem to end, sonny. Each day is fraught with tears. The weeping, relentless.

This sad, sad, letter, from many perspectives or levels is the hardest attempt I've made to tell you of my love, son. I have written some stuff before, but none takes the cake, or comes close to the wrenching agony of trying to put thought into word. Nothing. Strange as it seems, it seems to be the logical outlet for my grief and guilt.

Perhaps I pictured myself a scribe, son. I was published at fifteen and several times in academe. I did that because it was fun and exciting. From the "Oh Great Spirit" poem of a child to highbrow academe writing, it seems I have always wanted to write. But never did I imagine my greatest effort would come from your passing. Perhaps I was carrying forward our traditions of the learned, the intellectual, and the spiritual Odawa, Pottawatomi, and Ojibwe erudite.

What did Indians do before European script arrived? They wrote. They told stories. The oral stories were recorded on tree, rock, papyrus. The chosen form was through white birch bark although deer, moose, and rock inscriptions were common. They committed their lives teachings in all ways. But those writings have long been destroyed by the immigrants. And because most of our writings were on organic material and with no place to secure them, they have long since disintegrated, burned or been smashed.

∽

Born into the twenty-first century, we are products of the times, son. Born into the twentieth century we made it to the twenty-first. As limestone tablet and birch bark are no longer with us as the medium, we have adapted to western technology and print. We learned the Western ways, the decent and the bad, in the settler's format and forum.

Well, I guess I wanted to write, probably from watching my

grandfather read and write. I do not have a particular memory in mind, but I know my grandpa was of two worlds. He could read and write Western just as well as he could speak Nishinaabe. The Western and the Nishinaabe, or the Anishinaabe.

Old time's parchment or stone is still an option, but for convenience readily acceptable, technology is the way to go, as it will not attract the authorities and their well-meaning, but dumb, idiot environmentalists for example.

Did I ever tell you about the time some tree-hugger was telling a group, and I was the only Indian in the group, that cutting birch bark from the birch tree was killing the tree? Imagine that! Telling Indians that birch bark harvest was environmentally detrimental. These are the type of idiots I speak of, son. For millennia, we have built our homes, and pots, and utensils and tools for travel, and so much more form birch bark. This dumb white chick had the nerve. She and her like destroyed, and still do, entire forests. From my first days and into today, birch bark harvest has never killed a tree. I told her diaper-covered ass.

I digress. But these are people who cannot stand to get dirt under their nails or run from Smoky the Bear, haha! These are the people who fear the woods. They do not travel alone and must tame the wilds as they call it. I call it fear. These are the weaklings who like to stand on their soap boxes and dictate to our people how to treat the land.

Before I digress even further, any further, let me describe the environment we come from and inherited. Gramps would have loved to see you. He was of the old ways and he was an intellectual and farmer. He battled the government and took tribal politics to heart. He was an eloquent public speaker. And a scribe like I mentioned. He was many things. I was fortunate to observe him as a veterinarian, a fisherman, hunter, trapper, gardener, and he was able to locate underwater streams. He was also an herbalist for barnyard stock and for neighbors. He welcomed the thunder people each summer. He was a gifted man.

Somehow you inherited some of these traits. Especially strong was your ability to interact with the spirit world. I'll never forget the time you had fun scaring the crap out of your co-workers at Lake Louise. Mind yah, no one talks about this as it might be detrimental for business. But your workers regularly got spooked, especially at night. And you would have fun making noises or making strange sounds or just plain hauling stuff around to add a fright down their spines. Of course, you knew about the entities that resided there and how they travelled throughout the building. Poor white folk, eh. son? Nudge. Nudge.

The same work principle was alive, son. Not afraid to tackle hospitality at the front desk of the hotel or cooking in the kitchen. Certainly not shy to lead and get your hands dirty or speak your mind.

Respect was engrained in your twin daughters, Catherine and Chelsea. Your daughters. Love those gals. They are now mine, son. They remind me of my mother. So pretty and beautiful. And they have brains and just plain horse sense. They have your eloquence. They have the brains to rein in and dish out when necessary. Just like gramps. Yup. Gramps would have enjoyed your company then. But that was another time and place. That was my childhood.

I was fortunate to live on and off the farm. Wish you did, but farms had virtually disappeared from our family by the time you arrived. You would have seen my uncles and Grandmother work the land. They tilled the soil and waters. They scraped hides.

I can still smell the beaver hides hanging to dry for market. Uncle Alphie was the trapper. He was also the fisherman.

And I can still taste those giant Pike after grandma done cook them, son. Yum. What a prize. And I can still feel the power of those work horses in the barn. Such magnificent and intelligent creatures, son. The whinnying and neighing they call it, funny language, eh, son? Mixes well with the smell of horse poop shoveled out into the barn yard. I love the smell of horse poop. It's comforting for me to this day. I like the squish sounds as you walk in the fresh droppings. It's clean. It's just grass, son. Totally organic. Am I grossing you out yet, son? Haha. There are some things I do like getting into your craw about.

"Shut up, Dad!" I can just hear you.

It was these farm happenings that probably formed one of my positive attributes, not that I have much: writing, or the need to write. Many times and into the evenings I would watch my uncles and gramps read and write by the waning daylight. A kerosene lamp completed the evening. I remember watching them cut the wick so it would not make a twitching or uneven light. The oil in the lamp was visible through the clear glass from which the lamp was constructed. Whatever happened to those lamps?

Today, as my fingers fly and hunt and peck over the keyboard, I am reminded of those days so long ago. I do remember my gramps telling of many things that came to pass. He told of the moon landings and planes so big and so fast able to carry great numbers of people over the skies and get them to their to their destination that would take days or weeks by horse and wagon, which was our primary means of travel. No one ever doubted him.

That same speed he spoke of is evident today through this laptop. The pen has gone the way of the birch bark scrolls and limestone library. Or just about.

How about the time I wanted a pen so bad so I could write? My grandparents were going to some far-off exotic city and they were leaving me behind on the farm. I think I begged to go along. But to no avail. So okay, instead I pleaded for a pen. I cannot remember how I came to the idea of a pen. I was only four or five, if that. Anyway, I wanted a pen. Just like the grown-ups, I suppose.

I remember describing in great detail what this pen should look like. I went on with its description. It had to be a ball point pen with a special textured grip and color. Which color I cannot recall. But I described a thick adult pen with taper, color, and thickness. I think it had to be a ball point. I wanted a pen with dark ink. Not red or some other color. I was just an infant as you can see, but from somewhere, I knew I wanted to write. Come to think of it, I don't know if I was even able to write or print. But the desire was there, son.

So off they went, and I anxiously waited for their return. I think this may have been a two-day trip. I do not remember. But I remember the excitement and anticipation. Boy, this pen was going to be very nice I imagined. They arrived. But the pen did not. It did not arrive. They did not bring it. I cannot recall what reaction I had. If any.

Maybe this was when I began to shield my feelings and not let anyone close to me, or anyone I now ponder. This seemingly uneventful event may have been the catalyst for shutting down and not believing in anyone or able to trust. My evidence is, this event is one of the first and initial things I remember. The bad stuff. For me. Yes, I do remember the good, but the bad somehow stays a lifetime and twists and deforms. Maybe this was when I began to change into the dad that you knew, son. How is it that I was able to transfer this to you? If I did. If not.

"Excellent . . ." as you used to say after something worth laughing about crossed our realms. The mimic of Mr. Burns from The Simpsons was always worth its weight. Perfect.

Several lifetimes later, these same fingers hover and twitch over the computer. Shaky hands from age, shock, and gawd knows what else, search and crush the keys to create the longest composition ever attempted. Long in word count. Long in secrets.

"My fault . . . as well . . ." resonates.

Son. Shannon. Whatever fault referred, is a good step. The responsibility shows maturity, courage, and respect. For this I am happy. The "fault" tossed my way shows respect. Respect for others, self, and nature is a quality some never acquire. Respect was one of the qualities I think I tried to exhibit by example. I think I was successful. Was I?

I have no problem with taking my share of the fault. I blame myself for our shortcomings. Mine alone. Yet, no longer is your presence here to debate and argue and laugh over. We used to do that.

"Remember the time you wanted to become a priest?" you laughed.

"I did not," I denied.

"Sure ya did, Dad!"

"No way, son!"

I smile now. True. At one time I was in theology courses called deacon school. I laugh at myself now. What a dunce. They did not want me. I was not cut out to take orders. Or, maybe they saw I was not cut out to understand the Bible. I was too educated from a Religious Studies Degree at York University.

Anyway, it's a good thing I drifted away. I now can confirm there was no way I was made for that type of life. I'm too bad. "Bad to the Bone," as George Thorogood sings.

I saw George in concert, son. It was awesome. Wish you were with me.

"Gimme your clothes, boots, and motorcycle," the Terminator demanded. Haha! Again, you sounded exactly like Arnold. Man! You had a gift for impressions or whatever it's called.

I am so very sorry for not supporting your stage comic dream. I remember that time. What an idiot! You wanted to go up on stage and explore comedy. What was I thinking?! How super insensitive was that?! I later tried to make it up to you, and I think I apologized. But it was too late. The dream had been busted. By your own dad. What an idiot!!! That, my son, was totally, totally my fault. I remain ashamed.

I am angry at myself. I take full responsibility. If I had the wisdom, no, that's too much to ask for, the smarts, I should've recognized a child's dream. I don't know what my excuse, yes, excuse, was, and not reason, for busting your bubble. What an asshole I am! Still to this day.

So much I failed. Do not forgive me. I do not deserve forgiveness.

My failures originate from the rez life, son. Let me try to explain, sonny boy. I now know a few things, son, something that afflicted our families from 1492 with occupation, genocide, and the holocaust that spawned from Hispaniola to Wiky. If I grew up on the reservation, I grew up in a concentration camp. Just like any other Indian. Try to escape and you were shot, imprisoned, fined, beaten, and left for dead. The churches and government were in cahoots as they remain today. The military and the police are their agents.

This was the law of the land, son. Only recently we have fought back and regained our rights. But, do not be found in an alley with the white village people or the cops. For women, it's even more dangerous. Even today. I fear for your sisters and daughters, son.

These reservations were a garbage tract of wastelands the government and supporters did not want because they were deemed inhospitable tracts of swamp or rock that had no value. Read commodity. See. Everything is a commodity to these folk who do not know anything about respect for others or the land. Real estate, mining, oil is big business, son.

Anyhow, these tracts of land became home. Wiky was fortunate. It was deemed Unceded. That means we never signed it away. The only other Unceded tract of land is the Vatican. Which means we are a nation state. Ironic, that church land, the mecca millions of folks make pilgrimages to, is just like little old Wiky. But do not get too complacent, the federal government can make it all disappear with one stroke of the pen. There's that pen again. Maybe I was meant to do something with my pen, son.

This is where the reservations come from, son. Originally, they were created to keep us in prison camp. And to a great extent they still do by the nasty characteristics we developed from being closed in and unable to walk and talk with dignity. From this beginning, as good chattel and cattle, we were chained within the sentried walls of the rez. No wonder I messed up, son. As my parents and grandparents.

I still remember the white Indian Agents as they were called. Their job was to keep us imprisoned through food stamps, or in the earlier days, they tossed, and usually very late, I add, rancid meat and flour and sugar or salt. This is where our infamous fry bread came from. Fry bread is prison food. It is not traditional food for the Nishinaabe. Now it's killing us with the bleached, enriched, white flour fried in lard and grease. Can you say hypertension or diabetes? How about high cholesterol? Heart attacks? Obesity? Yet our people have forgotten, and think fry bread is a traditional Indian delicacy. I laugh.

"As if!" They say on the rez.

Anyway, I digress again. But so much must be said, son.

Back to the Indian Agent. Nothing could be done in or from the rez without the Agents' approval. So one had to beg. Kiss ass. What crap is that? These agents were always white. And male. A very paternalistic model and system they inflicted. White Indian Affairs assholes who doled out salt pork, flour and what not. Their might was in legislation and in the pen. The Agents I saw had the paternalistic, condescending attitude. Even as a child I saw through their arrogance.

Outside the concentration camp was the racism. I remember the fucking merchants follow my grandmother and me as if we were thieves. There was the priest who barged right into our homes without bothering to knock. They ruled with an iron fist. The nuns whipped us children with three-inch wide leather straps that were about one-eighth inch thick and eighteen inches in length. Like their garb, the straps were black. Many times, for infractions I cannot recall, I was sent to the office for a strapping. Funny thing, we got to joke about it later. The trick was not to give them the satisfaction of crying. But, I gotta tell you son, those things hurt like a son-of-a-gun.

The shit-heads liked voyeurism, it seems. We used to peak through the windows. Question. Why would nuns leave their drapes or curtains open just enough to see them undress?

Funny was their cropped hair they hid behind some white cardboard plastic material they affixed above their foreheads. Secrets were our way of revenge. I think some of them left Wiky because they got pregnant. They wouldn't screw an Indian. Not the women nuns.

But with their own color. The priests. They came and went. Along with their groupies, the brothers they were called. We can verify that these priests begat children with the nuns. White on white meat. I know of priests who sired children with our women.

Dumb. But lust is lust. I know about that. The nuns had already been in schools and their secret lovers, the priests. We know about this, son. The rez is a poor place for keeping secrets. Some of them asshole priests begat children from our children in residential schools. Many children are buried in unmarked graves throughout the country.

To this day it's a hush-hush topic. But our people know.

Stress in a fourth world environment is a killer. As is guilt. Release has to come from somewhere. So the brothers had their fun with the boys. Payouts by the feds have since been doled out. I heard the bribe was ten-thousand dollars for each adult. Kill the Indian. Save the child.

I could never understand this, son. Is an Indian not a child? Is the child not an Indian? I do not get it.

They hung Louis Riel in Manitoba. He tried to prevent the killings and imprisonment of men, women, and children. Abe Lincoln as President executed the largest mass hanging in Mankato Minnesota when he ordered thirty-eight hangings. They do not like to be reminded of their legacy, son. They now go on pounding their chests for democracy and equality and other such bullshit. I know you did not know that in Texas you can still shoot Indians legally because they are considered a war party. This legislation is still on the books. There's a town in Wisconsin or Minnesota where Indians are not welcome. I know of a man who would not get out of the car when he pulled over for fuel or whatever. His white wife had to cover the transaction. In South Dakota I saw a sign "No dogs or Indians allowed." Sure, the Indians seemed to have been covered or washed off, but it was still readable... Kill an Indian Save the Fish was a popular slogan in Wisconsin during the fish-Indian wars.

Arbor Croche Michigan was the site of one the first mass biological warfare attacks inflicted by the government. I think it was a distance of some thirty leagues along the shore line or so, that entire populations were wiped out from small-pox. It seems the Odawa were gifted with a small present at the completion of one of the heads of state meetings. They were presented with a small box and instructed not to open it until they arrived home. Inside was something strange. That fungus, or whatever it looked like, launched that pre-emptive strike against the Indians. Documented writings confirm the shorelines littered with disease-ridden corpses for three leagues inland. A league is about three miles.

Of course we know about the Wounded Knee massacre where the US army took out their Gatling guns on a sleepy village of Lakota peoples early one winter morning. Old men, women and infants were mowed down and unceremoniously dumped into a pit. Pictures exist. Photographed by the perpetrators. Certainly not the Indians. So no, they do not like to be reminded of their genocide.

On January 2012 in Shawano Wisconsin, a seventh grade school girl was kicked out of Catholic school, along with two others from the same rez, for speaking her Menominee language. I love our Nishinaabe women for taking lead. In Winnipeg Canada, a young lady was kicked off the city bus by the bus driver for wearing a shirt that read, "Got Land? Thank an Indian." *This was in November 2013!*

MacLean's magazine of Canada, in January 2015, named

Winnipeg the most racist city in Canada. On and on it goes. From 1492 when Columbus kidnapped the Taino Indians by the hundreds and took them back to Europe as commodities and payment for his financing. Again, if one could not produce enough gold, their hands were hacked off. Dogs trained to kill were unleashed. Conservative estimates of Indians killed across America are seventy million.

This material is all public, son, yet hidden from the education curriculum. I often wonder if those kidnapped bore children. As the rape of men and women was initiated by church and state. I wonder if those elitist descendants from the Spanish and others are part Indian. Haha!

I find my own particular fun, son. I often ask the Spanish or French what tribe they come from, as they are darker than me and look more Indian than me. I get a kick out of this, because I know they will deny any lineage. Just nice to see them squirm. They know that I know they lie and are indeed Indian, even though they try to portray themselves as French-Canadian or whatever.

After several hundred years of punishment and death, locked in reservations, we as a people turned sick. Who wouldn't? As my uncle used to ask, "What did we ever do to them?" except to save and cure their starving asses when they first arrived on Turtle Island. Nothing.

How did Germany start two world wars and not lose its land, culture, language, community like we did? How about Japan? How come they still have their country? Britain, France, Portugal, Spain should forfeit their culture and lose all their lands. They were the leaders in genocide on this land. That's what I say, son.

This is the legacy and environment inherited by your father, and just like you and every other Indian on this planet. So yeah, I come from wounded peoples. The boarding home syndrome has done its job. It has critically wounded the Indian. For the last one-hundred and fifty years, Canada and the United states financed the extermination of the Indian. As one woman said, and I paraphrase, "Terrorists with machine guns mounted on their boats came and stole our children."

Imprisoned children in boarding or residential homes across two countries came home not knowing how to raise and nurture children, because they were not raised with love but instead under the yoke and whip.

Inter-generational trauma is real. I know I am a product of this long-term death campaign.

This is the shattered man that begat you, son. Although raised in love and nurturing for the most part, your dad came to you in fragments. It's just that I was not fully aware at the time. It was some time before I discovered PTSD, intergenerational trauma, and cultural grief.

Recently, a boarding home survivor from home told us a story. She said, "Did you know that Alexandrine was the mastermind for escaping the Spanish residential school? And she was the one that got us back home to Wiky!" This lady was talking about your grandmother, son. My Ma was the mastermind! Can you believe that! How awesome is that? Your grandma led two other girls out of the concentration camp. My Grandpa hid her and made sure she never returned. By today's transportation, that is a good two hour drive by highway.

My mom never talked about it. Any of it.

Inter-generational trauma led to devastating consequences for our family. I know that it affected those who came before us and shaped their behaviors. Not for the good. Although there are those who claim nothing bad happened and it was the best thing that happened. Oh well. This may have been true for them, but my thoughts are, they deleted the trauma. The mind has a way of self-preservation.

Memory deletion does not mean one is free from dysfunction. I should know. I speak from experience. I do not remember how I may have been sexually abused. Nor can I say beyond the shadow of doubt that I was molested. Instead, I think about it, question, but at the end of the day, I can sense something terrible.

For years I have had the sensation of something trying to enter my anal cavity. And for most of life, I let it go and thought it normal. It was not until intense introspection through therapy that I discovered it may be a natural sensation or a body memory.

If abuse did happen, it had to come from someone.

Intergenerational sexual abuse usually causes the victim to inflict the same aberrant behavior onto another. And they in turn inflict others. And so the cycle continues. This is the nature of our people today. If it's not sexual, it's other forms of violence.

In my home it was my dad beating up my mom for the first ten, twelve or thirteen years of life. I was witness, being the eldest of nine. Sure they quit drinking by this time, but as I have said to others, it was too late. The damage had been done. If the first three years are the formative years, then I would have been programmed to beat up women and develop the aberrant views of them from then on and into adult life.

There was time when this nice looking lady was visiting my parents. When she went to leave and had presumably gone out the door, I raced over to the chair she sat in and smelled the place her bottom had been resting on. My parents were there and chuckled when I said something funny about her rear end odor. What made me do such a thing? How did I come to learn this behavior? I had to see or learn from someone. Right? Or was I born like this?

I do remember my mom saying she was not ready for me. I was still in the womb. It's not the words I may have understood, but I understood the feelings. I was not wanted. This led to a life of low self-esteem. Something I recognized in myself when I was on the cusp of my teens. I figured this out for myself. This memory also led to a life of womanizing. That is, I spent a great deal of my life changing girlfriends. Just because I may have seen this darkness in myself, it did not mean I was free of its influence.

I used to think I was hot shit, son. Several girlfriends always in tow and they in turn knew about it. Maybe they were doing the same. Whatever. This was my way of making myself feel appreciated. To feel wanted. What is that song by Aaron Neville about being a "deceiver"? That was me. And I was damn good at it.

I can say in my defense that I did not mimic my dad and beat up women. Whew! But I did abuse and misuse them. The shit that I was. Hot stuff! That's bullshit. On the contraire, I thought I was treating them good by treating them with food and company and, in later years, what I considered respect at the time. How is that for a dichotomy? There were times I had one in each arm, as it were, and jumping from one to the other, several times within the same day or twenty-four hour period.

I have reached some sort of awareness. It has taken a lifetime.

And it's going to take the rest of my life to crawl out from sick, abnormal behavior. Thanks to intense therapy and ceremony over several years.

Gone are the anal sensations. Gone is the womanizing. Gone are the lies and deceit. But I do have to keep a close eye on myself. I need to monitor myself daily. So far so good. My way of thinking and perception about women has to change for the better and find respect in myself and other human beings.

Family saved my buns the instant I was informed of your death. It was family that held me together. Family is anyone who is in the hoop and were there when I needed immediate help. This catharsis is the way for me to heal. I do not know if I am successful.

This battle for liberation is not new for you. You know all. You are in a place where you grasp all that came before and what will come. Our memoir may possibly impart some help for others torn up, and like me, during one explosion of desperation, may find something of some help. If we can reach one person, maybe our episode will have been productive.

5.

NNGII-SHKO-WAAS-IGE
(MY FIRE IS EXTINGUISHED)

I was returning from Wisconsin one April morning. With me were your siblings, Dave and Angie, and Dave's girlfriend. The girlfriend of your brother made up the four person ride. We had finished the usual ritual, breakfast and onward to the outlet mall. I stayed in the car and eased the driver's seat back to its full horizontal position. I also slid the chair backward to its maximum so I could stretch my legs. I folded the sunshade down, adjusted my sunglasses snug, closed my eyes and tried for sleep. I may have succeeded. I do not know. It was not long before the shoppers returned from their shopping. Tired, I asked Dave to drive. I slipped into the seat behind him. Traffic was moderate even though it was now early Sunday afternoon. Angie got into the front passenger seat while Dave's girlfriend sat to my right. And off we went. North was our direction and the Upper Peninsula was our destination. Small talk consisted of their spending and all seemed quite pleased with their excursion.

Comfortable at cruising speed, the discussion shifted to our collective lack of sleep. No one could sleep the night before. Not me, your sister, brother or his girlfriend. We agreed to share the driving as none of us were satisfied we were in the best condition. Satisfied we were okay for the moment, I decided to check my cell for messages. And you know me and my deafness.

I hate that cell phone thing. First, I cannot hear well, even in the best of situations. My hearing aids help to an extent, but I so dislike the continued interruption into my ever-so-hard-place-to-stay happy.   I reluctantly turned it on for a moment. Waiting for its burps and beeps, I finally entered my secret four digit code and waited for the obnoxious voice describing my choices and what not. Finally, I arrived. I have messages. Great. Going through the motions I deleted or ignored most of them. I stopped dead when I heard your mother's voice. The message was very simple.

"Kenn. Call me as soon as you get this message."

But it was the voice that had me come to an abrupt halt. I said nothing. The car continued to rumble up the interstate. As deaf as I was and as loud the construction and rumble strips, I clearly heard the weight and urgency in her voice. I think I briefly looked out towards the speeding traffic in the next lane. I had never heard your mother's voice sound that way. It was a heavy rasp. I knew something was wrong. I don't know if I checked for more messages or not, I cannot recall.

I knew it had to be early morning as there is at least a three to four-hour time difference between the Midwest and the Yukon, I almost wanted to wait to return the call. I did not wish to wake her if she was sleeping. I think I checked the time the call came in. The weight of her voice made me hang up and scroll down my contact list. I punched the automatic key. Waited. Then she answered.

Oh son, this was when it all changed.

"What?!"

She answered on the first or second ring.

As I could not hear well, I asked her to repeat.

We were on the rumble of the interstate. I was in the back seat. The roar of traffic on either side kept me from correctly identifying her words. Again, I asked her to repeat. By this time, I knew it was a grave situation. At one point, I was in disconnect. On another level, I knew she had to immediately deliver bad news.

I remember Angie turning around and I saw that cloud of shock begin to form across her face. At the same time she had a questioning look. What? I repeated what your mom said. Simultaneously, I was begging in some obtuse way that I was not hearing right and the message was not the one I heard. I crushed the phone deeper into my right ear piece.

"What? He did not survive?! Who?! Karen, I cannot hear you!"

I was behind Dave as he was driving. And Angie's upper body was now contorted towards me. The look on her face told me she knew something was horribly wrong.

"What?" she seemed to ask.

"You are telling me he did not survive? Is that correct? Is this what you said?" I tried to enunciate clearly.

"Who?" I shot back in shock, question and disbelief.

Even though I thought I didn't understand, I fully comprehended her words. I relayed the shock almost verbatim. Maybe for my own assurance and total belief setting in, I responded.

"Shannon?!"

Angie's jaw dropped and her face went pale. We locked eyes and I saw the first sign of mist gloss over her eyes. Mine probably also.

At this point I am sure everyone in the car knew something was seriously wrong, son.

I felt the car lurch into the exit lane. I was still talking to your mom. I do not know how much later, but I felt the car exit onto a ramp. I slumped towards my door. I kept pushing the cell into my head. I don't know what else I said, if anything.

My immediate concern was for your mom, son. No one else said a word. I repeated what your Mom had just delivered. All in the car heard. Dave launched onto the first available exit. The next thing I know we were twisting this way and that as we negotiated the streets. He then pulled into a driveway and came to stop. We were in a residential neighborhood. I was still holding on to the phone and must have hung up at some point. I knew I had to relay the news.

"Shannon died last night. He died in a snowmobile accident back up north in the Yukon."

And the rest was shock, disbelief, and intense sadness I have never felt. A numbness seized my body. I sat immobilized.

We were sitting in someone's driveway. We were in the States. We were in Wisconsin. And I knew they shoot people there. Indians would not be a problem, was the thought going through my head at the same time. The rest was shock.

I still heard the echo. "He did not survive the snowmobile accident. He was a passenger."

The conversation replayed itself in my head.

"I don't know what to do!" your mom sobbed.

She asked for help. She was crying, son. Mama was crying. I held myself together as best I could. I also knew she was alone some two thousand miles away at home in Whitehorse, son, and there was not a damn thing I could do for her. I felt useless.

As we sat in that stranger's driveway I thought, what if someone comes out of that house and shoots us? That's what I thought, son. I was thinking of your brother and sister. What if they don't like Indians? Or, what if a neighbor calls the cops and have us arrested for some stupid thing? All this was swirling in some confused and shaken matter inside my head. I do not know how long we sat there in that driveway, son. There was no one about. No one on the streets, walking or otherwise. Nor were there any dogs barking. It was all strangely quiet. The houses all seemed empty, as if no one was home, even though they had trimmed hedges and green lawns.

I was vaguely aware of Dave exiting the car as his girlfriend followed. Some inhalations later I followed. Dave was sitting on the back of the car's rear bumper. The trunk was open. His head was down. His hands were on his knees. No one was talking. No one spoke. It was very quiet. Your brother had not said a word. His girlfriend had her hand on his shoulder I think. I returned to my seat.

I sat there immobilized. The news that hit set in deeper as the numbness began to occupy my body and senses. I held on for stability. No matter, it was intense. I could feel my back and neck seize. My breathing stopped. I did not cry.

Dave appeared with a burning stick of sage. He held it in front of me. The smoke was thick. He was offering a smudge. Automatically I hovered my hands over the smoke. I washed with the smoke. I rubbed the smoke onto my chest, head and arms, son. All the while, I worried about our safety.

Though it was a bright sunny day, I was still anxious about some redneck or cop coming over to seize us as the smoke from the sage could be mistaken for weed. Some might think the burning sage was a doobie.

Somewhere deep inside, I was impressed that Dave had the gumption to bring the sacred medicine.

Thank you, Shantu, for keeping everyone at bay while we took turns cleansing ourselves with the uplifting smoke. Not one person walked by. Nor did anyone approach. It was as if the day stood still. And no one else could enter.

Unbeknownst to me, your brother travelled with the sage. I did not. I did not have anything. None of my ceremonial equipment was with me. I had come for a break. And I did not want reminders of all the times I used my eagle and goose and assorted tools of prayer and help. Dave had retrieved the sage from the car trunk at some point and lit it. Without that help, I cannot confirm I would have made it back. Again, at some point, he extinguished the sage. I saw him return it to its container pouch. Awesome. A tear rolled out.

Repeating what I had said moments earlier, I said, "Shannon was in a snowmobile accident last night and he did not survive. He is dead."

About that time that Angie allowed herself to gasp, I think. She cried. As a dad I had now delivered the final verdict. I think I had to repeat it two or three times.

"Aambe. Let's go," I pronounced. "I'm driving."

I drove home, son. It was the only thing I could do. Reach for some control I guess.

We changed drivers at a service station just meters from the Michigan state line. Angie wanted to drive. I then replaced her on the passenger seat. This semblance of frozen control disintegrated when my sister Bea called bawling.

"Your son! My son!"

That was it. In less than a minute, I broke down. My stomach quivered, heaved, shook, and my chest caved in. Unable to hold it together, the flood dikes broke open and I bawled with her. Too much sorrow to hold. The shock flooded out. I released a torrent. There was no stopping it. With the phone shaking at my ear, I heard Angie, "Dave. The tissue."

A wad of tissue came from Angie. I took it. It was like trying to halt a raging river. The dike had been breached. The proverbial flood gates were open. I shook and sobbed like a child. Each tissue dissolved in the torrent.

The torrent continued with your other mother. Auntie Bea was always there for you and you two developed a very warm relationship. You spent many hours at her place. Someone from my family loved you and took care of you and your cousin Chris. I knew you were in good hands. The love got to the point where you called her Mom. This love was the old way of indigenous raising of a child. "It takes a community to raise a child" theme has recently found its way back to Native America. For this I was happy.

Here she was calling from Chris's home in Phoenix, Arizona where Chris worked as an engineer supervisor. Both were a mess. Your Auntie was sobbing uncontrollably. And I was on the highway. Somehow, I found it in me to walk her through her grief. Next was Chris. I could hear him barfing in the background.

"He was my brother too." He cried.

Son, these were the initial moments of shock and total, utter despair.

I had now talked to those closest to you. It was a mind numbing and excruciating task. And this was only the beginning.

A day or two later, I remember Uncle Mart came to visit. He fondly recalled all the times Auntie Bea had to talk to you and even discipline you along with Chris and Dave.

"He always took his medicine with the boys," he smiled.

"He never once shucked his mistakes," continued Uncle Mart. "He kept his head down in total acceptance. He took it all. Just like the boys," he added. "I thought that was pretty good of him."

"I remember him riding the lawnmower," Uncle Mart continued. "And you know, he was always shirtless. And barefoot!" No matter what, he was out there in the full heat. And his skin always had that great bronze color."

I can picture you, son, riding out there doing what had to be done. Might have been later a few times, but I was always proud to hear you pulled your own weight.

I suppose this is the reason Chris asked you to be the best man at his wedding. All of you in stove pipe black hats, tails, and white canes. What a sight! That was beautiful.

I remember the time Chris was waiting at the Phoenix airport and getting them and everyone else all worried. Being a no show was not cool, son. No calls. No text. I thought that was not being cool at all, since they bought you the ticket. It was later we all discovered you were in the drunk tank. Fitting! It was also at this time I discovered they bought you the ticket to get you into rehab.

And you decided the night before to go out and get drunk and cause a ruckus. Dumb you, son. Not bright. Not smart. Not mature at all. Had you maybe been in rehab, maybe your life would not have taken such a drastic turn. Who knows? Maybe it would not have made a difference. That's all in the past now. Nothing we can do about it. It's a part of your legacy, son.

It was a long ride home. It was also very quiet. The radio was off. No one spoke. I don't recall if Angie and Dave switched driving. I sat there weighed down in my seat. My crying had ceased. Bea and Chris were left on their own. At least they had each other, I was thinking. Me? I felt so numb and alone at the same time. I was so distraught.

We arrived later that night. I trudged into our apartment. I immediately sought the battered arm chair. The kids were milling about. One of them brought me a photo album. I don't know what the first picture was I saw, but the next of you in your top hat and tails from Chris's wedding was the one that finished me off. I bawled uncontrollably. I don't know how long I sat there. At some point, I bawled out, "Is there no one that can fix this?!"

I was a zombie. My limbs and entire body weighed tons. I could barely move. Again, I do not know when, but I retired to my bed. I laid there in numbed shock. I laid motionless in the dark. I also cannot recall if I had the sense to slip on my CPAP. I gazed into nothingness.

I replayed the talk I had with my cousin Martha. She and I had grown up together and were close in age. She was the one person I called soon after I saw your pictures, son. Martha. Dear cousin Martha also lost her daughter to cancer only a couple of years before. What I replayed over and over in my head were her words.

"Kash-ki-toon gwa."

She was offering her undying support in my moment of need. Her love was genuine. Her tears touched me as her grief was very recent and raw. She was the one I thought about soon after the news, son. She would know what to do, I figured.

I remember getting angry during my long-distance telephone conversation. I was angry on many fronts I suppose. I was angry that she could not fix this. Yet, I knew, deep inside, no one could. The irrational part of me thought all of this, this death, as fixable. This was where I also asked for my mommy.

"Help me please."

"Daddy, help me."

Dear cousin Martha went over and above to comfort me.

"Ngii-kendaan. Ngii-ken-daan ezhi-we-bak."

She was telling me she knew what it felt like. She was my first lifeline, son. She knew the horror of losing a child. Faye was only in her thirties. Just like you, son. Same age. And she was a mother.

Somehow words fail. But in another sense, at some other level, they comfort. After all, this was something I was grasping. Something that would make sense of this nightmare. In essence, her love and words did reach some deep, inconsolable quagmire of a place I never knew existed. She was my rescuer. And for that, I will always and forever be so grateful—that words and actions of gratitude seem so very futile.

Was Faye there to meet you, son? Does it work that way?

"My mom must be baking pies for them," Martha continued. "She's probably cooking up a storm for them."

"'Chi-jii-baa-ka-we-dik,'" she mused. And, "Debbie gayii 'Chi-naa-damaa-ge-dik,'" she chuckled.

She was referring to Dubbie, as Dave used to call her, when he began to speak as a child. It was a name that stuck with her. Martha was referring to the feast Auntie must have prepared to celebrate family home. Of course, Debbie and Faye would have been there front and center with help and laughter.

I even wrote a poem to dear cousin Debbie sometime back after her demise and got it published. It was my way of saying, I am sorry Debbie. I was sorry for not being able to do more for her. Debbie was born developmentally challenged, was the only one who bought educational, fun, and practical gifts for the family, son. Not bad for someone labelled "less than." Very noteworthy for someone who was both challenged and independent and who had to live with Auntie all her life. I think she was born gifted.

Auntie Josephine used to love cooking. "Aaniish naa geyi-Shannon?" she used to inquire about you, son? Auntie Josephine was the last of my aunts. I loved her. And I miss her company.

She was there in her sparkling clean home anytime I dropped in after some of my walks up in the bush behind her home. I remember scaring her once when I left my car there in her driveway without telling her. She almost called the cops she told me on my return. She laughed.

Now, here I was. Alone in bed. Frightened and numbed out as any father could be, fumbling for comprehension. I think I was under a blanket.

I remember the cold draft moved from my toes to my head. Exhausted, I noted the draft, unafraid, but aware that a cold breeze swept over me. I thought I had left the window ajar as I am prone, but I was sure that I had slid it shut before I laid down. Unable to sleep, the sensation tossed in my head. Back and forth the question went. Did I or did I not shut the window over my head? Not only was I too exhausted to check the window, but there was a part of me that succumbed to resignation. I did not care. These types of events were not unheard of in my home. This type of experience was nothing alarming.

And I knew you were looking out for me. I felt protected. But I also wondered if that was you, Shantu. So, as drained as I felt, I knew I had to know. I reached out and up from my bed and past the blinds. Sure enough, the window was closed tight.

"Cripes!" As you used to say.

I was now faced with another question. The question was, did my boy reach the other side? Or was he stuck in between? This question would remain in my head and I realized the enormity of trying to fix it soon. For the moment I was powerless. Unable to do anything. I must have dropped off to sleep at some point because I woke to pale light outside my window. All was quiet. I stirred and began to ask myself if I indeed felt the cold draft. Still horizontal and not wanting to get up, I slowly came to the realization that I indeed felt the wind. Cripes again.

Now you had me worried, son. In-between worlds is not where you want to be. I had to do something. Somehow, I worked myself out from bed, must have made coffee, and then picked up my cell phone.

"Aanii." Hello answered my friend Lloyd.

"I've a favor to ask you, brother," I replied. I then went on to tell him about your death only the day before, which now strangely seemed so very long ago. The ragged tear in my heart and soul confirmed, yes, it was only hours ago.

I went on to tell him about the draft. And I asked him to check for me if there was a problem about your trip home. I asked for immediate remedy. He was back home on his rez on the north shore. I mumbled something about my concern and that you may have not reached home, or heaven, as others call it. "Waa-ka-wiing" is its proper name. I asked him to tell me what to do, if anything, to fix the problem, if indeed, this was the case. No way did I want you hanging out between worlds and being miserable, son. No way! My job as dad was to still guide you. And by gar, that was my job.

"Alright," he said. "I'll get right on it and make a fire."

That moment brought immediate relief. I knew you were in good hands, son. Lloyd is like a brother, and I trust him with my children's lives.

I was fraught with anxiety not knowing if you got home safely. I did not want you wandering the Netherlands. This was the drive behind my request from Lloyd. I wanted assurance you got home safely, and if not, I was taking measures to make sure. This included the making of a fire and having a sacred pipe ceremony. Now. No later. Not to be delayed.

"My brother," Lloyd told me later over the phone, "I do have something to tell you."

I held my breath. "I made the fire and prayed for you and your family. I also asked for help for your boy. What was his name?" he asked.

"Shannon," I answered. Shannon Meawasige from Cutler."

"Ahh, okay," Lloyd continued. "Well I made the fire and asked my people to check in on him." I listened intently. "Your boy thought he was still alive. He thought he was still here. He kept going with the good times. But he's okay now. He's reached home and is with others and his family. He's okay. He now knows he's home. It's all good."

I nodded. Relieved. Out of deference for his help, I am sure I muttered a "Miigwetch."

As messed up as I was, I truly comprehended the significance of his words and the information they carried. He was not done.

"I sat next to the fire and made sure all was good, and continued to be good," he went on. "As I was minding the fire and sitting next to it, I heard a lil' something behind me on the tree." He was referring to the large poplar tree immediately behind him.

"Before I could turn around a woodpecker landed at my feet. A big one," he added.

I said, "Aanii" to it.

"I knew he was the one that made the sound. I have never had a woodpecker land at my feet before," he continued with the story.

"It just landed between me and the fire." I listened intently. I may not have been breathing. He continued, "It was one of those big ones. You know, the kind with the big red plumage on top of their heads. Papase."

"Holy crap" began to form in my stressed mind. I took it all in. I may have said something like, "Okay, keep going." I waited.

"Yeah, so this Papase was just walking around the fire barrel. And he walked once around my fire." Lloyd makes his fires inside an old rusted fifty gallon metal drum that he had burnt though with a torch and cut the barrel in half. And this was his fire site. His alter. His sacred site. Many times, we had sat together with the fire over the years.

"It came right up to my shoe and made a poke at it with its beak," he continued.

His voice slowly shifted from the serious, to the lighter version. He chuckled. "A couple of times. And I was sitting right there on my chair. He wasn't even scared of me or the fire. Never saw this before," he emphasized.

"And he even looked up at me and then my shoes. I kept looking at it and said, Welcome. Stay awhile. It went to the barrel and tapped it with his beak a few times. The heat did not seem to bother it. Nor the fire, brother." He coughed to clear his throat. "It circled the hot barrel and just kept walking around the area and returned to my boots. It kept looking up and around the fire. It would tilt its head up to look at me every once in a while. And I just kept looking at it, smiling" he added.

"I knew it was good. It was a good sign. That was his dodem," he instructed. "Your boy made it across. He's good now. And he also told me to tell you not to worry. And not be sad."

I lost it then. He waited. Patiently.

I fell down inside at that point. That is the only way I can describe the sensation. I dropped. I fell. I collapsed. Inside. Meanwhile I was still sitting or standing upright. On so many levels or maybe only one or two, I died and collapsed, again, or deeper, yet rose to the sky with the eagles. And the woodpecker, Papase.

One, I was relieved you made it home, son. And two, I now knew your name. This was the name you came into the world with attached to the cone head birth. You were born Papase, right down to the shape of your cranium. My God! I do not know if I cried over the phone, but I must have and profusely, between sobs, thanked Lloyd for his work.

"No problem, my friend" he replied. "I'll keep an eye out for a while yet. One more thing," Lloyd added. "Out to my right and behind that tree line, towards the south, I heard his buddy calling him. He was calling out for his friend. I couldn't see him but I heard him somewhere in those trees. And just as quick, the Papase responded and looked towards the call. Up and off he went towards the sound. And he was gone.

"Yup, he tilted his head and lifted his head, sat there for a second, and was gone. Off he went to join his friend." Satisfied he had explained his episode as best as he could and reassure me, he finished with his story.

He asked, "How's that sound brother?"

"Whew!"

A brief light pierced through my dark. And that was good. It was a great relief knowing you were home, son. What great relief. Even though the immense load I was carrying was lifted for just for a moment, I will never forget the story. From the innermost sanctum of my being, son, I took that moment to relay with the deepest heartfelt appreciation I could muster.

I was also relieved knowing I would not have to find a way of sending you packing. You had to go home. And, cripes, I was not looking forward to any further effort, as I was extremely taxed. I was unsure whether I could do it. It meant more fires and just plain old work.

Miigwetch for finding your way home, son. I miss you.

ᔕ

And that is how I came to discover your name. Papase. Ahh, the richness of that name. The depth and breadth of it, sonny. The

Papase is a messenger. An intermediary. And who cannot miss a bright, bright crimson-colored messenger? And one who knocks to enter. No other bird has this ability.

That was you, son. One of a kind. You are Papase. And you are the bird.

Your plumage shone often before and after the event. Always in a manner one could not help but notice. Your tales, I may have thought of them from time to time, or they scared the shit out of me, I add, exhibited a larger than life series of events. Each tap for each story sang a message, son. All were for a reason, or reasons, unknown. Now, you are gone, but your knocking has touched everyone for life. None will forget your frolic. Very few did not like you. Otherwise, everyone liked you from Asia, to Australia, to the Yukon, British Columbia, Alaska, and other points I am probably unaware of, to home on earth in Wiky and Cutler. You were one of a kind, son. Forgive me for sobbing as I write, son. Ha! Fuck that, eh, son? Let the old man cry, eh, son?

Papase we call this bird. The name describes his characteristics. He likes to bang his head against the wall, or the tree. That is where pa! comes from. And because he repeats the action, he does another pa! And so on. This action and sound gave Papase its own distinctive name. I know you did not know that, son. Now you do. Because we are a damn creative people and our language and song is ever so descriptive.

The Nishinaabe describe what they see and hear from nature. This etymology is the framework for our language, son. Conventional orthography recently developed has replaced the pre-contact expression of script and communique. Almost totally gone are the petroglyphic styles. As English is now the predominant language for communication in Western society, some idiot has come up with other ways of writing an oral language. So they came up with the common alphabet applications and developed tools and the writing for oral sounds. One of them is the double vowel method that seems to have found application through the Nishinaabe speaking world.

"The hell with them, Dad!" I can just hear you, son. "First they beat the language out of us and now they want to write it?!"

True, son. There is a reason for my madness. Hang on. Just

bear with me okay? Let's break down the word. Okay? The "Se" is multi-leveled. As is "pa." Each syllable tells book length stories. Which I do not want to explain. You're welcome. Okay, change the "p" to a "b" sound and again, the description changes dramatically. At the same time, the "p" and the "b" sounds are related in tense, past, present, future, singular, to plural, to the collective, and what they call the animate to the inanimate. Silly folks, eh, son? There is no such thing as inanimate. Nor are these two sounds closed to further applications. And that is only the "p" or "b." Never mind in a string like Papase. Put any two of these syllables together, and again one has multiplied the applications exponentially.

Never mind the interpretations, or the dialect. So much to tell, son. But Papase, the bird of that visit, would come to be your name and your Dodem. The Western term of totem is erroneous. Even Dodem can be said the same. Dodem is my clan, which again is too simplistic, nor is it spelled correctly, if one wants to follow their idioms, idiots, haha, I make myself smile, but they are trying totem, which, again, follows what I just explained, but for the sake of convenience, totem, is now synonymous with clan. Whew! Got that, son? That is only my preface, preface to the prologue. Haha. Let's get away from that, son. Moving on ...

Be that as it may, the Papase was a major player in our lives, and deaths. And post-death. Grandmother Laura tells the story of your visit with her in Toronto. I think it was the night of your leaving. But I think it was the following night. Anyway, she was sitting in her comfortable sofa chair in her home. And I paraphrase.

Before her appeared this young man. He was dressed in old regalia. Old style clothing made of hide. He was beautiful. He shone. His eyes were like the stars. And his skin was of bronze. The power he embodied was not of this world. He appeared before her. He was standing a few feet away. And he was facing her. His presence was undeniable. She went on to describe his headdress. This young man had the brightest red headdress she had ever seen. The headdress was all of bright red plumage. Just bright crimson. As he stood firm before her, he took a step forward, knelt down on one knee, took her hands in his hands, and leaned into her. He spoke secrets. Grandma Laura does share the gratitude this young man expressed to her.

In her words, "He was a young, tanned bronze, lean and muscular, very strong young man with so much love. He expressed his deepest appreciation. Then he was gone."

The next day she happened to tell of this visit to one of her daughters. She could not recognize this young man, "His face was not clear."

"That was Shannon!" her daughter answered.

Almost immediately, the visit reached my ears. And for that, son, I thank you. Thank you for visiting Grandma. She was the one that paid the largest amount for your travel from Vancouver. Your body was still waiting for autopsy. And it was Easter weekend. Everyone was away and it was a long weekend with the Friday and Monday off. The coroner's office was closed.

And when it did open, there was a backlog from the long weekend. And you had to take a number.

"That was Shannon," her daughter had revealed. "That was Kenn's son."

Your visits with Grandma Laura and others as Papase now made complete sense. Miigwetch, my boy. Miigwetch for putting it together for your Daddy. Miigwetch, Ngwis. Miigwetch for that visit.

Together, the two visits confirm the other. Both happened mere hours from the other, across a distance, and hours after your travel home. Grandma Laura is a strong practicing Roman Catholic. Lloyd is a traditional healer who accepts his responsibility and keeps his distance from Christianity. Grandma Laura is on the cusp of ninety years of age, and Lloyd is close to middle age. One lives in the city and raised her family there, and the other could not and does not want to ever live anywhere else than the rez. He raised his family in on the rez. Both are so very spiritual. Both give with their hearts. Both spirits are independently strong.

Perhaps you chose to visit Grandma Laura as she was the one that put up the cash along with your mother to bring you home from the coroner. I can see why. Grandma quickly and without question offered cold hard cash to bring you home. Your mom maxed out her credit cards at the same time. Lloyd was responding to a request. For free. Without charge. Without asking for anything in return.

∽

It was a big old red-headed woodpecker who foretold of your leaving not too long ago.

This huge red-headed woodpecker came to land on my driveway pole. Irritated by the damage he was causing, I got off my lazy ass and went out the back door to chase him away. Gingerly, I went out the back door and eased down the porch. Took a good look at him and decided he was in no rush to move on. He seemed quite happy to chip away at my fence pole. I remember thinking, what the hell is he going to find in pressure-treated lumber?

Pissed off, I searched for some rocks from the gravel that was digging into my bare feet. I located a couple that would do just fine. I made sure there weren't any pedestrians or the sound of cars approaching, I heaved the first rock. Missed. Didn't even phase him. He kept pecking. Hmm. Checking again for traffic, I heaved another rock. Again, I missed him and the fence. Irritated that he was interrupting my morning coffee, I searched for another rock. Found a larger one, tossed it, and hit the wooden slats in front of his pecker. Bang. That did it. Off he went towards the east. That was the first and only time the bugger visited my yard. Satisfied he was gone, I returned to my day. He was a nice looking woody with a bright red crown with black, black plumage that shone in the morning sun.

Who knew of the impending future not more than a year later.

Shannon was a child of nature. Like his Dad, Shannon slept on the herbs and grasses amid the shrubs with total abandon. Shannon was comfortable outdoors in any season. With his dad, Shannon dreams of plant medicine in the fields of Wikwemikong Unceded Indian Reserve.

Shannon Meawasige reaches for his offering. Shannon was taught to give thanks to the stone and rock people that live with the grasses, trees, and the spirits, that would come to hugely impact his life. Here he is with his dad and teacher, Kenn Pitawanakwat.

Time out for Shannon Meawasige and dad Kenn Pitawanakwat. Even Spiker Pete joins in the foray. Shannon is taught about the strength of one tree over another and how the Nishinaabe are dependent on them. In this image, the tree people, the four and two legged, the young and the old, share their inter-connection within the change of season's and the never-ending Medicine Wheel.

Photos by Allan Joyner

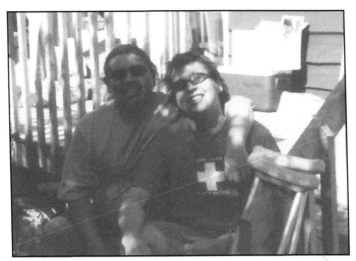

Shannon Meawasige was encouraged to take risk and not be afraid of challenge. Here, Shannon sports a reminder for his humility training. Challenge, yes, but always know Mother Nature is the boss. Shannon sports an injury from tumbling off a mountain. Dad, Kenn Pitawanakwat, is happy just to have him alive.

Photo by Lorraine Pitawanakwat

Photo by Karen Meawasige, Victoria Day weekend, 2009—"We were heading up to Dawson City, YT. We stopped at this Historical Site. It is called the Montague Roadhouse. Well, it is all that remains of the roadhouse. It's a beautiful picture of a beautiful person."

Photos by Karen Meawasige, Victoria Day weekend, 2009—"We were travelling across the 'Top of the World Highway' from Dawson, YT. We planned to drive through Alaska, then back to Whitehorse via Beaver Creek, YT. When we got to the US Border, we had to turn around and drive back to Dawson because it was not open yet (we were one week too early). This is Shannon's sad face at the news. Then one of the guards came out and let him 'cross to the other side' and it made him happy!"

6.

NNGII-CHI-BAA-BII-CHI-GE
(THE AGONY)

I was staying with the twins' grandmother. Grandma's everywhere, huh, son? I was a mess. I really do not know where to go from here, my boy. All I knew was the constant phone calls with your uncles and mother and my siblings. And I was cold.

The twins' Grandma's house is a cold drafty place built sometime during the last ice-age. But I did not complain. Grandma welcomed everyone with open arms, hugs, food, warmth, and love. For this, I remain eternally grateful. I was not on the street.

This was during the long weekend. April 18th. It was now seared into my mass of crumbling or mush brain cells. My memory was shit, son. Everyone was on hold. Your Ma was still in Whitehorse. Dave was on his way to Seoul, South Korea. Rose was in the Caribbean with her fiancé. Ang was in Wiky. We were scattered all over the planet. And your wii-oh was either still held in Whitehorse and later transported to Vancouver, and lying on a cold slab somewhere deep within the bowels of an inner city morgue. Christ! It was grim.

If the accident happened on Friday or early Saturday, all of us were now exhausted. Painfully slow, that weekend turned into Monday, then Tuesday, then Wednesday. Each day we held our breath. And no one was answering the phones in the morgue.

Your Uncle Dennis was point man, son. Love him. We agreed to not bother your mom with chatter. Dennis would be the only one to talk to her directly. All of us waited for any updates as he kept in touch with the Royal Canadian Mounted Police in Whitehorse. So much he did, son. Each day was torture. Each day dragged on. By Wednesday, I think, or was it Thursday? Dennis received confirmation that you were ready for transport. The autopsy was complete. Exhausted and relieved, the final arrangements could proceed.

Your mom could now move ahead and arrange for own travel. Dennis, who is a great man, took over the Vancouver funeral home arrangements. Next was bringing your Ma home from Whitehorse.

I did nothing, son. All I could do was nod, look, or listen to the latest updates.

By this time flight arrangements were complete for your mother and your body. Donny, my first cousin, who works with funeral homes was there for me. I specifically asked for his help as I knew he would provide the family touch, and he knew the intricacies of funeral home arrangements. He was my designate. Someone from your mother's side of the family decided your wake would only be one night. It would be at home on the rez. And this was fine by me.

The decision for the one night visit was because your body was too long in waiting, even with refrigeration. We now were into the sixth and seventh day. The norm is three nights with burial on the fourth day.

I was just a walking zombie. I smoked a cigarette almost every couple of hours or so it seemed. This behavior was new. I prided myself for not smoking until I was a late thirty-something. During high school, I smoked once or twice and did not like it, as it hampered my running in track and cross-country which I loved. It was as if the lungs could not take in as much oxygen, thus shortchanging my short legs.

Plus, I was not sleeping. So when the decision arrived for only a one-nighter, I felt both saddened, as I would not have as much time with you, yet relieved as I knew your mother and others must be just so exhausted. At the same time I was respectful of the family wish. I, too, was just so extremely drained.

Amazing to see what the body can take. Its motor and direction can be seriously compromised. But I kept upright when required, son.

Looking back on that Tuesday with the first full day of work after holidays, it continued to look grim. No one from the Vancouver coroner's office could provide a direct answer. No one knew anything when you would be sent home. The best answer was, maybe, just maybe, by Thursday. This reply did nothing to ease our pain. Tuesday turned into Wednesday and everyone was anticipating a better response. Again, the morning brought no relief.

Sometime during the day (or was it early Thursday?) confirmation was received that you could be released for the trip home. I am sure it was that Thursday, because we buried you on Saturday. Right? Why does it matter anyway which day?

I can hear you in the background, "What's it matter anyway, Dad?!"

True. I guess. But some things just have a way of nagging.

I was just relieved the backlog of autopsies from the long weekend were caught up. So when the word finally arrived, your Grams, Uncle and mother, made the final details for your final trip home to Cutler.

The undertakers were ready. One to pack you up and get you out of Vancouver. And the other to pick you up at Toronto International Airport, then drive you back to Sudbury in a hearse. From there, the hearse would bring you to the community hall, and after that one night, take you to the Sagamok crematorium. And from there I would bring you home to Momma and family. This part was going to be my job. No problem!

The Band Office had been cleared. When I got there I was told the Chief and Council had closed shop for the day out of respect for you and your family. Like everyone else, we waited for the hearse arrival. I was a mess. I hate waiting. It kills me. Friends and family began to trickle in, some of whom were from Cutler who I had not met. Your uncles took the lead to do what they had to do with the community and its leadership. I love them all.

Up to this moment I thought back to the days prior. So much to recall and so much a jumbled mass. Perhaps, one of the good and positive things that stood out was the awesome experience with Lloyd, son. Martha was divine. Each had their place.

Then you arrived. We watched the hearse reverse to the main entrance as the building's two doors were wide open. The back door of the hearse lifted. In there was the box. Donny and the undertakers directed the traffic. They rolled the box out of the hearse and onto the lift. They then rolled the box into the facility. You were in. They rolled a careful left and into the meeting hall.

Someone had put up the backdrop for the casket. Donny and assistants took the time to delicately situate your coffin. They then asked for direction. I do not know if it was me or someone else, but

I was there with your mom, the twins, Grams, and your uncles. I do remember facing the casket and looking down at it. The twins I knew were not doing well. I took each by the arm and had them on either side of me. I made sure I had a firm grip on their waists. I knew the shock of opening the box. I knew what to expect. Or thought I did. On cue, I think it was me, I nodded, "Nahaw."

The lid lifted. At that moment you came into view and I heard the collective cry and gasp of shock from Catherine and Chelsea. We froze.

All of us stood transfixed. Your Ma, Grams, your girls, and uncles.

The attendants went respectfully about their business of opening the lids that lined the top half of the casket.

We had not budged.

We stared. We could only look, son. And the rest is a haze. The next thing I noticed was the pungent scent of burning sage and the cloud of smoke coming over all. It was Barb. She was smudging the casket. We remained standing, I think.

The girls were sobbing and I began to shake and not doing well trying to hold back the wail. At some point the tears arrived.

But I do remember Barb back behind the casket and doing a complete circle around the casket. In her hand was the sage bowl and in the other, a large eagle feather fanning the smoke. I had not even noticed her beforehand. She had come up from her home on an adjacent rez. She was there for us. And so was little Carson. He was her assistant. I think I may have smiled to see him there, performing in such a grown up fashion. He might have been ten or eleven. He was following Barb with extra sage in case she needed more. At some forgotten point, we all took turns approaching the casket and the remains of our boy and love.

I was a bit disappointed to see your hair gone from view. Most of it was hidden as a pony tail. The other thing I noticed was the bruising that the off color makeup could not cover. Face and hands looked puffy. Even in death your hands exuded the strength of a strong man. The left covered the right.

I sort of remember the shirt mother had selected. I think. I think it was the long sleeve black with a red bear paw over the heart. The same tattoo over your back shoulder. It was our reminder of your inheritance and direction. It was Manido. No wait. Someone changed their mind and instead picked the white satin ribbon shirt tailored by one of the community. Yup. I think I can almost be sure. That was the chosen top. In the end someone chose the white satin shirt, I think, with ribbons.

We still had our backs to the group. At some point, we must have turned towards the mourners. I was still holding your babies firmly in my arms. And I said something like these are your daughters. It was the introduction of your children to the community. And I was damn proud of them, son. And by inference, my pride in you and their mom and everyone else that had raised them from infants to mature and brilliant women now in post-secondary studies.

"They are now my girls."

I was sobbing through very direct announcements. I said, I am taking your place.

"I shall now attempt to raise them. I shall be their dad and not only their grandfather. I do not know how successful I will be, but I will continue to do my best. That is if they allow me."

This adoption was my way to get over my guilt for not being there for you, and them, I suppose.

There was a time over the years I used to say with great admiration for those raising children, that I was all burnt out from raising four children and no way could I ever find the energy to repeat the process. That was gone. It had left immediately. When, I do not know. It was at some point that your leaving for home meant the girls needed you now more than ever. And you were gone. Someone had to step in. And that job fell to me. It was my duty to step in and help with the grief, and the future. I did not know if I could do it, but I knew this would be my last job on earth. Gone was the hesitation or fear to raise children. They were now my children. And I was going to do it until they no longer wanted my help. I hoped that day would never come.

So there it was, son. I had the Indian way of adoption. No papers. No bullshit government. All I had to do was announce it and it was done. The old Indian way. We are shining beacons of carrying forward our traditions, son. Are you not proud of your babies? They still want me and kiss me and hug me whenever we meet. I know my time is short on this plane, the clock is ticking, so I do not mince words with them. After all they are adults and know the ways of the world.

Oh, the usual. Guys and what they want. The only thing they want. And I made sure they knew what I was talking about, and they knew. I talk to them like adults, son. Later I would go on to help them with simple but efficient self-defense maneuvers.

Do you remember Al, son? Well he was at the wake as my support. "Weird Al" as you used to call him at which he only could shake his head.

Well brother Al was there for us, son. It was during my vigil in Wiky that I had called him to tell him the bad news.

"Shannon died," I had told him over the phone.

My memory is blurred, but in that day I called he had left his company immediately, went home, and packed his camping gear, and left with a call to his wife Michelle, that he was on his way to Wiky, an eight hour drive. We later learned that Michelle gave him some sort of heck, as she wanted to be with us also, son. Pray for them both and their girls okay? Anyway, I was at home on one of these days waiting for your arrival, and had left the Soo at some point. It was nighttime. A knock on the door. Who was there? Al! It was Al, son. I immediately broke down, hauled him in, and gave him a crushing hug and kiss on the cheek, and muttered something like a thank you.

What I do remember is his response, "I would have been upset if you had not," he said in reference to the phone call. He was there in eight hours. He took off for Wiky the moment after our talk. And he did not tell me.

I did not know of this, son. It was a total surprise. Allan was there with us in Timmins back in the late seventies. He saw you grow. And we were colleagues in audio-visual production. We go that far back. So for him to show up was an ultimate gesture of respect, love, and support.

At the wake he was there as my brother. Even though he's white as they come, which is a common theme in our diatribes, Al takes it all. I think he was the only white guy at the wake. In fact, I jokingly remarked to the mourners during the opening remarks to look for the white guy as my support and confidant, and not to withdraw from him. Chuckles and smiles spread across the room.

Al knows the Indian ways, son. He knows the elder and community protocol of respect. I taught him. And we still have fun with that. He now is looked at as point man and the first step in to a community, whereas his production crews are uncomfortable with Indians. So they shove him to the front, to get the ball rolling. He brings gifts and offerings.

I did not know this till later that day or so, but he went to the trading post for food or whatever. Someone behind the cash register asked him who he was and where he was going, you know, the usual banter.

"Oh, I'm here for Shannon Meawasige's wake and funeral."

The gentleman behind the counter promptly dropped unconscious. Imagine that! Not everyone knew of your demise. Even on your rez. Wow!

The sandwiches, coffee, water, and juice and the help that went with it was plentiful, son. The community did a beautiful job of feeding a small army that day and night and into the next day. We appreciated the smiles from the kitchen help. People I had never met. No one went hungry or thirsty, son. And the children frolicked freely up and down the stage, kitchen and outdoors. Me? I stayed glued to my seat save for the occasional visit to meet and greet as it was, sandwich or drink. Not that I had to get up that much, as people known and unknown, family and community, young and old, brought me food and drink.

Catherine and Chelsea remained standing. We had not moved.

"Shannon brought us together by dying," I said. I continued, "We are strangers. All of us. Even with family. We are too busy with life to make time for another. So Shannon's death as I see it, is his way for us to join and meet and get to know another." And I am at fault. I am number one I said.

"I want you all to first come up here and introduce yourself to family. " There was Mom, Grams, and your uncles sitting in the front off to my right. "This is Catherine and Chelsea. And when I cue, I want each and everyone in this audience to come up here and hug the Shannon's family. Tell each one who you are."

They followed my direction. I had taken the twins back to

their seats, and I stood there to oversee the introductions. And I told everyone not to expect the family to stand up. The onus was on the mourners to initiate respect and condolences.

When the circle of condolences and greetings of sorrow were complete I then continued with my theme.

"Now go and hug that person in front or beside you. Tell them your name and where you come from. And give them a hug. Not a handshake. A handshake means nothing. And smile." And so being the shy Indians they were, they reluctantly moved around and made that effort.

"Remember, this is what Shannon would have wanted. Everyone to be happy."

In essence, son, I took advantage of the situation. But, it was not for personal gain. It was for love. For everyone to get reacquainted, and make new friends, and take the nervousness out of the air. It worked. People broke into groups and were chatting. This included the children.

I hate funerals and wakes for this reason. They are too stiff. It's too clinical. Gone is the warmth and laughter and the share of food and memories and stories. This is why I did it. I did not want your wake to be remembered as another uncomfortable time, but a time of laughs and conversation during a very dark period. This is the traditional way. Another one we got away with, son. I later heard they wanted "a traditional wake and funeral" back on the rez as a matter of course.

I was not planning a "traditional ceremony," whatever that is, son. Things just happened naturally. The only traditional component was the fire in the teepee just outside the doors. This began with your family. The wood, teepee, and the fire keepers were organized by your uncles, son. So they got it going through the entire time. It was all good. Right on.

"Carry on chap!" as you used to say.

I never did once go out to the fire, son. I was just too stunned. And I was happy to see the effort. I do not know who was there. I kept indoors. And I sat vigil. Every once in a while a good waft of the burning fire crept though the hall. And this was comforting.

I had brought my lawn chair as I knew there would probably not be any comfortable chairs. So there I sat the entire time. I slept there. And I ate there for the most part. Much of my cousins from Wiky were there. Cousin Margaret brought one of daughters. She was there for the most part and I took the time to visit them. Chippendale and Misty and their four or five little ones were there from Michigan. I was quite impressed with that young man. They made that entire trip. And they stayed the entire time. Their kids running around and making noise and mischief added to the family and home feel. Nishin was there. Uncle Dennis and Uncle Kurt and Uncle Ken gave me a sense of acceptance. Auntie Charlotte came and covered me with a blanket she had brought one of those times I had fallen asleep I my chair. All your family was there, son. It was a sad time, lightened by love and support. Thank you, God.

Auntie Bea and Mart could not be there as they were in Phoenix. Kitos was there in their stead. Auntie Kathleen was there too. Cousin's Chuckie and Brandon were there. Charles looked so adult. Uncle Herman and Rachel had travelled up from Lansing. Rachel travelled with her Dad along with her brood. I was pleasantly impressed. They made the effort. Everyone was there when it mattered.

Every once in a while I would make the rounds and visit. I tried to smile. And show my appreciation and love. I tried, son. But I would also go up to the casket and stand or kneel in front of you. Did you hear my words?

You were my boy. You were my son. And I had no idea what to do. I remember laying my head on your chest and holding your hands. I knew you did hear me. I asked of you one request. I asked you to take me off Paxil as I now was up to three or four times the dosage. I was tired of it. I was tired of feeling numb from the medication. I had begun taking that stuff some twelve or thirteen years ago for anxiety. I think. I cannot remember.

I wanted to feel normal. I wanted to feel free of dependence. I knew the pharmaceutical was doing its job, but it swung way too far to the other side of feeling distant, cold, unattached, and groggy in the mornings. I used to take it at night before bed. Now my schedule was thrown off, as I had been going without sleep for a week.

"Help me, son. Help me get off this stuff," was my request. As exhausted as I was, I knew sleep would now be elusive and taking drugs would not help. Nor would I need medication for anxiety. Nothing delivered anxiety like a child's death.

Anything, everything else I might come across in life, would be nothing. I had suffered the most devastating and anxious moment in life. Drugs were no longer needed. I no longer wanted them. Good-bye. Au revoir. So long. Sayonara. Git! As of this writing, I now am pharmaceutical free. Good riddance!

And that was that.

The pre-visit of your death was not forgotten. I made sure everyone knew the Papase visits. I told it in all its color soon after we opened the casket. I had also made sure that I had brought enough bright red cloth. I can't recall if it was the first day or the day of your final leaving that I had the girls, Mom, to don the red cloth. I had previously cut it into five or six foot long lengths. Each was about six to eight inches in width. I do remember the day you were leaving telling all concerned to wrap the cloth around their heads in remembrance. This was for Papase. And more importantly, for you. When it came time to close the casket I asked each to place their plumage on top of your forehead and drape the rest lovingly across the width of the casket. We all took turns. Catherine Chelsea and you, Mom, I do recall fussing with the cloth with great attention and love. The cloth was now you the Papase.

Papase was also your name. In honor of that relative and in honor of your memory, I announced your name sometime during the proceedings and how you came to be named. The name you were born with, the character and personality now made sense. You were a runner and announcer, and able to see things not of this world. You were quick to see through façades.

Uncle Wayne I want to mention. He was there. Along with his partner Charlene. He provided the resilience for my family, especially for Uncle Duffy who long ago was labelled challenged. Duffy came with my sister Millie and her husband Cho-boy. People say she looks exactly like me. Millie and Cho-boy provided the impetus for thinking of my dad, mom, and grandparents and all my other cousins. Millie has the maturity to comfort. Cho-boy would do anything for another at the drop of a hat. So, it was good for me to have people I could count on.

Cousin Martha could not be there as she was busy with another death in Orillia. She would have been a big help. But it was good enough I got to talk to her.

Kitos tilted her phone over your body in the casket during the final hour, son. She was bringing live coverage to your Aunties, Bea and Kathleen, in Phoenix. I remember the horror and shock across their tear-drenched faces as Kitos had me talk to them face to face. Your second Mommy was present that way. Words that may have been exchanged are gone. Kitos reassured me that she had not recorded. That's a no-no.

It's a no-no because we do not photograph or record spirits. It's disrespectful. It's culturally inappropriate. It's rude. It's dumb. So I was relieved to know that Kitos was respectful. Mosho, she and Chris used to call you. How did you ever get that name?

Dave could not be there with us. Yet he was. The eagle feather that carried him through his darkness was now in your hand. Your left hand was holding it upright. In honor of the eagle, as our relative, intermediator, and protector, I was proud of your brother for handing it to me as he said, "Give it to Shannon."

And so the eagle arrived. The lone feather, it chose to manifest itself as all beauty, power, the beginning and the end, sugar-coated with infinite love for its own, and to remind us we would never be alone. It gave us the strength and the courage to carry on with our place in the universe. The eagle came from the infinite, a place we call home.

Each and every one of us would part the fauna hide that separated our wiigwaam from the next-alone. Once we stepped over this threshold, we would be one. We would be joined as family and have the total and complete answers for our tears and joy. We would arrive home. Just as you did, son.

I knew this as I touched your hands, arms, cheeks and hair. I hugged you. I cried. Alone. No one there could say or do anything to lift or remove the crushing sorrow. I felt so very alone. I could only lay my head on your chest and hold your cheek. That was all I could do. The feather's power could not hold back the sobbing.

At the same time I was mindful of my surroundings. Family and friends milled about. I did not care what anyone said or saw. I did not care. I was your dad. I was there to sob over my dearly departed boy. I had every right to do what I wanted. When I wanted. For as long and as often I wanted. No one dared to disturb.

I don't know how I survived the cremation. The eagle feather had been removed and given to your mother. She was the one that suffered the most. Your mom had sacrificed the greatest gift and possession. She gave up her own flesh and blood that she carried in her womb. She was the rightful keeper of that feather.

To burn that feather would have been the ultimate no-no. The feather and the bird were both sacred and a memento of lost love. The feather was now Shannon and held his spirit. Your spirit and the feather were now one.

Remember the time a winter bird landed on your head and shoulder and ate from your hand when you were out winter camping off Point Grondine? The rest of the Wiky crew could not believe it. How long ago was that? Twenty years? But here you were and the blue–gray bird appeared out of nowhere and chose you.

I remember your story and how everyone was just amazed and you took it as matter of fact. The photograph speaks to the event.

You were of the winged totem.

Now you were to fly away that morning. The red cloth strips had been carefully arranged across your temples to commemorate Papase the bird and your name. You were now going to fly with the eagles. They say, the bird that flies the highest is the one to oversee its feathered cousins and the folks who were their soulmates. Fly away, son. Fly away.

Al, Ang, Catherine, Chelsea, your Mom and uncles Bob, Kurt, Ken and their spouses and families prepared the final moments. I think I may have said something before the box was sealed. I don't remember too much beyond that, save for the waiting for Chief and his honor drum song group. Donny continued to lead. Barb smudged.

The click of the casket sealed your final exit. The box was then led towards the doorway. At that moment the most beautiful and soul piercing sound of a travelling song began. This I do remember. The sound. The song both pierced my heart and uplifted my spirit. I was proud of my boy. I was proud of my heritage. I was proud of the Chief and his group. I was proud of my girls, my new daughters. I was proud to have my son honored with a song that would carry him home.

The drumming and singing continued as we led your casket. A love of pallbearers carefully guided the casket through three doorways. The first two from the building itself. And the final door of the hearse.

Then the hinge of one of the casket handles broke off. I was shocked. I was standing right there. At that moment, a memory of my paternal grandmother's burial sprung to mind. On her way from the funeral home, her hearse got into an accident. Some car t-boned the hearse carrying my Grandma. I remember the fear.

"No!" I shouted to myself.

It was good that the top third of the casket was already resting on the floor of the hearse. And very fortunate the hinge did not break away from the assembly in mid transport from the casket carriage and the rear entry of the vehicle. I had visions of you falling out of the casket and the horror it would bring to the bereaved. My mind, as dull as it was, had already visualized what I would have done to gather you up and cradle you in my arms, as we would fight to upright the casket and put you back. I could only try to imagine the cries that would have sprung up from your babies, Grandma, Mom, and everyone else.

I think I drove myself. Or I think it was Angie that drove. I think it was Angie. We followed the hearse.

Am I imagining? Did we drive around the village first? And did we deliberately slow down in front of the home you grew up in? If so, we did. The caravan of mourners slowed down on Canada's major highway as if to say so long, until we meet again.

"Baa-maa-pii miinawaa ka-waab-i-min." In essence that is what it was.

It happened, or a memory from too many wakes and funerals from my life, came to haunt. The hearse or the vehicle carrying the deceased to the graveyard makes a final tour of his home, family, and community. Any travelers or vehicles approaching along come to a halt and pull over. People in their homes or businesses stop to take pause and respectfully bow their heads or observe the proceedings. But things do stop. Just for the moment. After the hearse and lead family transport have passed, activity resumes.

I have seen this too many times. I know at least a hundred community members who have died. Many of them were relatives. Some were acquaintances. Some were strangers. But we all know, with too much familiarity, the feelings for death and its reverberations. No one looks forward to a death.

When a death hits a community, everyone feels it, son. There is a pall of heaviness, weariness, gloom, and darkness that permeates the air and entire population. Even the dogs howl. When the dogs howl, it's both frightening and unnerving. That pall lifts after the burial.

Several times I have been pall bearer or cross bearer. And several times I have lowered the casket into the ground. You never want to let the strap escape from your grip. So, we always made sure to have firm grip from everyone. One slip and the casket could drop and tumble open. Horrors!

No wonder I went into some type of anxiety when one edge of the casket handle ripped from its mooring.

The ride to the crematorium was only about twenty minutes. Sagamok Indian Reserve is the only reserve in Northern Ontario to have such a facility. We arrived a few minutes behind the hearse. Lloyd was standing outside waiting for us. We hugged and exchanged respect and just plain happiness to see another after so long an absence.

Again, why is it that we only spend time with one another at wakes, funerals and weddings? Something is wrong with society. This is not the way it is supposed to be, son.

But here he was. He led the way into the doorway. Since no one was at the front office, we walked towards the rear of the building. This building has a comfortable looking sofa and chair to balance the office and business end of death and grieving. We reached the crematorium.

The crematorium is another first experience. I have never been in one or near one. They always abhorred my senses. Strangely, this time, it felt non-intrusive or foreboding. The smells normally associated with death and embalming was absent.

The building itself sits beside the Spanish River. Got knows how it got that name. Did Spanish explorers get this far north? Doubt it.

It's more of a long rectangular building with one or two chimneys protruding from the roof. Inside were the fire chambers. The first one we saw was dormant and no one was there. Through another door we entered. There was the incinerator lady. She saw Lloyd first as he was ahead of Angie. I brought up the rear. I think.

Of course Lloyd knew the people. After introductions the lady nodded and tactfully stated that most people were normally not allowed in this area. She went on to explain meltdowns. It seems this is where most family members of the deceased fall apart and added to an already stressful episode. Understood. We described our tears had gone dry for the moment as we were now into a full week of emotional trauma and quite ready for the cremation. Lloyd confirmed. With that being said, she left us to wait as she disappeared into the next room. A minute later she returned.

While she was gone we chatted and studied your casket. It was sitting on the roller platform thing.

When the attendant returned she made small talk and was assured meltdowns could not be possible. She then turned to the furnace. We watched. She flipped a few switches and buttons. The furnace kicked in. She made some tweaks as she adjusted the temperature and stood by to see everything was in order. The furnace hummed, roared, blasted and we could see flames through the little observation window on the steel door of the stove. She disappeared again.

We sat there, looked at each other, and observed. Small talk continued. She came back a second time, did some adjustments, and again disappeared. I think it was the third time she seemed satisfied all was set to go. She then walked to the casket and took hold of the rolled cart holding the casket. I wanted to ask if she needed help, but decided against the question. I think Lloyd might have asked. So we continued to watch the proceeding.

She rolled the entire ensemble to the front of the furnace and adjusted the height to meet the gate. Do I have this reversed? Did she first roll the casket in and then flicked the switches and adjusted the temperature to 2300 degrees?

I did ask how long the procedure would take. Two or three hours for the burning and another hour for cool down. At 2100 degrees I think. There's a meter we kept an eye on. It seemed to settle at 2100 degrees.

This was a first. I never had witnessed a cremation. Much less for one of my own. We were pretty calm and alert with the procedure. I guess I was also relieved another one of the final steps was taking place.

She saw Angie and me peek through the observation plate window. She advised it was not a good idea. Lloyd said he had seen those corpses sit up in the fire. I did not want to see that, so I resigned myself to my lawn chair, the same one from the wake. I sat adjacent to the incinerator.

I do not think I left the room. Again, I was there overlooking the comfort of my son. Maybe I did leave, as I do remember Lloyd describing how he had seen birds fly over the chimney and just disintegrate from the blast furnace heat. And I do remember watching the earth-colored smoke blow out of one chimney. No birds flew by.

I think we did have a smoke break or two. Angie was talking to the attendant after some point. She later told me the attendant was intrigued with her forensics education.

Lloyd stayed by my side the entire time. He didn't even sit. Calm as one can be that dude. Eventually I did peek through the window and could see flames just churning up the remains of the casket and your person, son. Inside the furnace I saw a large lump or clump of darkened black mass with flames blasting out from the length and depth of the fire chamber. I was okay. I knew it was the body withdrawing from its transient state. As they say, back to ash and dust. I was also okay to know your life spirit was long gone. It, you, had gone home to its continued spirit and spiritual realm. You were not of the physical anymore.

We stayed with you to the end, son. Some two hours later, the attendant flicked a few switches, knobs, diodes and what not, and turned off the furnace. We would wait for an hour or so for the ashes to cool. We waited. Patiently. Outdoors it was still daylight.

In the facility we killed time by studying the two incinerator rooms. I think we walked back and forth a few times during the process, and finally decided they were of the same size and probably of the same brand. It was something to do. Just glad it was not in use. We liked having the place to ourselves.

For that we were thankful, as our time alone during the ceremony gave us time to catch up and develop a deeper and richer relationship between us all.

Lloyd has been at many wakes and funerals on the rez. He's been at the incinerator several times. He is one of those special human beings placed on this earth to help the human with the spirit world. He was telling us that at times he has seen the deceased walking about the crematorium looking lost. There was nothing he could do for them. In your case, this was not so, he shared.

Because we had lit the sacred fire, the power released led the way home.

The power of fire, semaa, and asking for immediate help and strength was irrefutable.

For this reassurance, our undying gratitude to the powers of the seven directions would not slip away as long as our blood and memory and tradition remained. As long as one of our dependents was alive, Shannon would not slip away from memory. Not you, son.

The ultimate power of semaa and fire and prayer had done its job. The ultimate despair of lost direction, and wandering lost in cold and darkness had been successfully avoided. For this knowledge, we were happy. Happy as one could be in these excruciating circumstances.

We talked of these. I don't think we said too much about you. Or to you. That would have interrupted your tasks because we knew you were doing what you had to do. And we did not wish to impose. Lloyd being Lloyd repeated, "He's gone home." He said. "And he's good. Very happy now, Very happy."

As if we forgot. Or could forget.

He meant well. And he was showing his love for the family. And his every gesture, smile, and word were welcome, as we knew this incinerator business was only fleeting, and we would have to travel on our separate trails. Again. So we made the best of it.

One more thing I will say about our friend is he did not pretend to know what we were going through. He did not say, "I know what it feels like," as I have heard some say.

I knew darn well this was not the case. Their words stung, stabbed, and the wound bled. And they had no idea what they were saying.

"Okay, let's check," said the attendant.

We stopped dead in our thoughts and discussions. It was time to see if the remains were safe enough to handle.

She donned a pair of gloves and reached for a flat metal shovel-type scoop. Nothing too technical, I concluded. No special tools. Just a plain old scoop and everyday work gloves. She opened the door and it swung open. It did not make a sound.

The plain old scoop was of the long handle type. Then I think she had a hoe type metal utensil. She reached in with this hoe and began to pull toward her and the door. Unbeknownst to us there was an opening that ran almost the width of the door just inches away from the door seal. A small plume of ash jumped up as she pulled the first scoop towards and into another unknown receptacle below this slat opening. We heard the scrape and the soft thud of ashes hit the metal container. There was the occasional clang of metal hitting metal. One of these was a cylindrical container of two or three inches in width and about the same depth. I remember seeing it in the casket. It was somebody's offering. I remembered it being reddish with some design. It now was a twisted piece of metal. We continued to look.

I do not know how many minutes we watched the lady pull and drop, pull and scoop, and towards the end, gather the remains into a clump by the drop opening and finally drop that clump into the metal container. I think she also had a wire brush also of about six feet in length to pull the finer grains.

I took a peek. I saw the walls and floor of the blast furnace were gray from ash.

I think she banged each tool a couple of times inside the furnace before she gently leaned them against the cinder wall next to the furnace. The attendant then might have said to look out or something like that as she was following through with the next step. It was also cue for us to step back and not get injured from the next step. I retreated a few steps and might have sat down.

With finesse, the attendant then clicked something from the front and below the same door your coffin had slid. She then closed the door. And from under the door, she extracted a metal tray. In it were your ashes, son. The tray looked like aluminum. It was about the same width as the slit and approximately ten inches deep and about a foot in width.

She grabbed the metal handles from each side of the tray. She then walked towards us two or three steps, and turned to her left and straight onward to a metal table next to the back wall. This table had a matching pre-designed drop. She put your remains down. She then adjusted her grip on the handles and flipped your container over and a small swirl of ash jumped upwards.

"Now, we'll give that more time," or something like that she said as she removed the gloves and retreated back towards the office. "I'll be back."

Left alone, we looked at one another. We were steps from the stainless steel counter. I strode to the counter receptacle and looked down. My hands were by my side. I stooped over to get a closer look. I felt a degree of heat on my face. Careful not to get burnt, I withdrew my head and shoulders, just as Angie and Lloyd approached.

"Wow," I thought or said.

It struck me. All we are is a mound of ash. Nothing more. Nothing less. Just soil. Or ash. The ash did not look like Shannon.

This observation must have gone on for some time. Not too long.

The attendant's steps returned from the next room. We stepped back.

She retrieved a gadget of some sort from the area and talked over her task. She plugged it in to an electric outlet and began skimming the tool across the sand and silt of ash. We saw what she meant. It was a magnet for retrieving any remaining metal parts from dust. With each skim we saw metal screws and such from the casket dropped into a separate container just off to her right.

She flipped another switch and the exhaust fan on the wall sprang to action as she continued with the metal search. A mist of fine gray soot rose from the ashes each time she ran the magnet over the pile. That switch opened up an outlet that led outside as I could see the shrubs and trees outdoors. The metal slats from the grate stayed open until the end. That was when I noticed the fine gray dust from previous work that covered the pulley, motor, and general work area. I had not noticed earlier. I was a bit inquisitive about this observation but decided to keep quiet. At any rate, she continued until she was satisfied anything metal had been extracted.

Complete, she gathered the ash with a small metal utensil. With a series of scoops she deposited the ashes into a square, dark container which I now only noticed. This was the lot of you—physical and holy. No longer were you the child I raised, but a transformed entity.

I am not sure what else beyond sadness I felt as I watched your remains scooped into the dark plastic container. It was essentially a black plastic mold. I was sad and a bit unnerved when I noticed your ashes mingled with the rest of the ash powder that was there. I was sad and protective at the same time. And I did not want to leave any remains. As the container was full to the brim and capped off with a square black plastic lid, I knew the practice of some residue left behind was common for cremation. I never realized until then. One cannot scoop every grain of dust.

We followed her out to the front office. She was carrying the ash container.

She produced some papers from her work desk. The official variety. She sorted them and explained each document and the need and line for signature. She kept copies and gave us our copies inside another official typeset envelope. Inside were the papers for your flight home back to the Yukon. Your mother would need these at the time for air travel. Adhesive labels were peeled then affixed to the dark container. With that complete she handed over the lot. The envelopes and ash remains. With the container warm from the heat from your remains, we walked out the door and into the parking lot.

Lloyd and I exchanged some parting remarks. Al had left for home before the cremation. Angie and I were left to carry you home.

Al and I began our work together as an audio-visual team way back in the seventies for a Nishinaabe political organization. Later on, after broadcasting school, we became business colleagues and produced several projects independently and collaboratively for assorted groups across Ontario.

Before your arrival in Cutler, son, I had asked Al to photograph images from the rez. He later made the digital album. I asked him for copyright permission. He answered, "No problem. Do with them as you wish."

This is the kind of friend I have, son. And he was there with us. I'm sure you saw him and know this. I mention it as a reminder more for me than for you. So I have those pictures, son. They are general images of the rez and fire lodge. Nothing intrusive.

Lloyd went on to serve his people.

Your baby sister and I returned to Cutler with your ashes.

S

How do I describe you and your life's achievements? I don't think I can. At the very outset, the father of two beautiful girls, the oldest of my kids, and certainly cousin, nephew, and only son and child for your mom. To your granny, a grandson.

The remains from that circle were enclosed in a plain dark plastic container. I held that container as if I was cradling an infant. As if you were a baby, I cradled and held firm to my boy on the ride home to Cutler. To Mom's and Grandma's home. The plastic was warm as your spirit, mind and body used to be when cooking elaborate meals and skiing extreme terrain. I would have liked to have seen you hurl down avalanche snowcapped mountains, my love. My fault I missed that. But I did see and hear the need for food variety, color, and balance, when applying culinary skills.

"Dad, it has to be visually appealing."

My mission was to bring you home safely. My job was to deliver your remains to your Mom and family. They waited at the house. It reminded me of all those road trips we used to take. My job as the driver was to get to our destination safely. In later years it was your job to help us take care of your siblings. First it was Angie. Then Teresa and then Dave. I still have photographs and slides and even some videos, I think, of you and the family.

In these last few moments, I was trying to make up for some thirty-eight years of abandonment. I deserted my baby when he was about four. But on that day, on that final road trip, I was determined to safely deliver. If this was my last mission on earth, by god, I was going to get it right! I was attempting to be the best father, protector, and teacher. In all those things I failed miserably. My fault!

As in those few hours at the wake, I did not leave you alone. Who would desert a defenseless child? I sat there. In vigil. Vigilant. Too little? Too late? I was attempting to reconcile three decades of neglect. I left you. And you left your girls. I am very sorry for giving a bad example. That is not a father who is loving and considerate. Love you, my baby boy. I always will. And I feel sad every day. And I cry. And I always will.

∽

What kind of sicko deserts their child?! Easy, me. But how did I get there? What made me into this monster? I have questioned my behavior. And the only possible replies, not answers, that explain some things, seem to come from witnessing my Dad's fists fly and the terror I was subject to before birth and continued ad nauseam into my formative years and beyond.

I heard and felt too much fear from the womb. From this fear grew frustration, and the need to referee adults when they were having their quarrels. What kind of load is this for a child? I'm sure it broke something. In me. And in my parents. Ma and Pa. Mommy and Daddy. I think it set the tone and templates for life. No wonder I morphed into a twisted individual.

No wonder, fear was always at the forefront of my experience. Later to exhibit itself as anger or rage. But guess what, son? I kept it hidden. Just as I cowered in my hiding hole, I hid my true self from others. These fears and angers would manifest themselves in all kinds of sick thought and behaviors. I was the happy and go-lucky individual in one phase. Then I would turn into the tough man or jerk in the next.

Especially after adult age arrived. I was the manipulative one. I seemed to get whatever I thought I wanted. I was the hunter. I knew my terrain and the creatures. I studied their trails and condition. I think I was a predator. Just didn't know it.

I would lure them in. And pounce. Bang! Done. What needed to be done was done. I was a fixer. I had a way with words. I would play that game. Listen. Nod. Or shake my head in disbelief. Usually, all of this action was for women or booze. Anything for a party. Man! What a shit I was.

Thank my maker for waking me up. Miigwetch!

I had the best training, sir. In real life and real life conditions. My training lasted for at least a dozen years. It ended only after my folks quit drinking. Too late. The damage had been done.

This is the skillset I did not want to pass on, son. Nothing to be proud of. I wanted to be the best parent for you. I wanted to be the best Dad. I did not want to be like my dad. I did not want to expose you to violence. I did not want you to fear life. I did not want you to fear men. I did not want you to exploit women. I did not want you to mimic my behaviors. Was I successful? Maybe. To some degree, in some quarters.

I confess. At the same time I am taking responsibility. I am accountable. I take my share of the illness. Willingly I will face my maker some day and say, "Yes. I did do this." Or, "No, I failed to do this."

As if, eh, son? That's the Christian influence. I know. I totally absolutely know, this is not what happens after we die. Your story is an excellent example.

Whatever. I digress. Or, off on a tangent? My son, I love you. Shantu my boy, here is my story that may explain some of my aberrant behaviors. I say "may." I don't know. But do know I am not trying to give an excuse. None of that! Just a soul-searching contemplation. Because the pain is real. Let's try to get back on topic.

We were talking about the womb experience. Yup. True. Before the womb was the world experience you now are in residence. But that's another story. Let's get back to the womb. My mothers' womb.

Strangely, the memory seems odd. Am I also questioning the memory? Maybe? Am I making it up? Possibly. I don't know.

But here I was enclosed in a soft pink hue. It must have been good for a while. Because the pink seems comforting. And it's a warm nest. I felt safe. I think I smiled once or twice. Maybe.

But all this changed when I felt and heard I was no longer wanted. From my mom! In her defense, I want to say, she was too young when she had me. Exactly nine months after her marriage to my dad. She was the only girl in the family. I do not blame her.

This was sometime after October 1951. But I do not know when my parents married. But I was the product of a married couple, born in 1952. So . . . their wedding photograph depicts a summer wedding at the old homestead in Rabbit Island.

That's the part of Wiky I never took you, son. It was the last farmhouse on the road. And our means of travel was on foot or horse and wagon. So . . . again, did they get married in the fall? But their photograph seems to show a bright sunny day. Without any winter apparel. Except for my grandma who was wearing a fairly heavy fall or early winter full-length coat. She did not strike me as being very happy in that photograph. But my mom, and everyone else, was smiling.

The whitewashed building in the photograph was my grandma and grandpa's home. This is where my mom grew up and posed on her wedding day with my dad and with their one bridesmaid and best man. This was where I also grew up to a large degree.

This is where my uncles lived and worked the earth and set fish nets along with birch bark collection, sales, and exchanges between neighbors. This is the place for humongous draft horses used year round for pulling earth plows, boulders and the log sleds my uncles made. This was the place we yelled out from on New Year's Eve as three shots volleyed from a 30-30 or 303 rifle. This is the place of the root cellar built out from a mound next to the tree line edging the fields of hay. This is the place where I used to watch my uncle Alphie scrape beaver hides he captured from trapping. This is the place where I used to enjoy eating the largest pike I had ever seen. This is where I used to watch my Grandpa sharpen his scythe and axes and knives over a large spinning wheel that bathed through a wash of water to keep the stone clear of grit and fine metal dust. This was the place for awesome home-cooked meals always ready and prepared by my Grandma.

This was the place of my first theft. This was the place for my first cigarette. I stole the DuMaurier cigarettes from my grandmother's package. And for which I got some talking to when I returned home to the village proper. That in itself was a good three hour walk.

This was the place where we literally hauled up water from a well which my grandfather located through the use of a fresh sapling. Amazing to see, actually. More amazing is the ability.

Just as amazing was surgery on pigs and other farm animals without the benefit of formal education. And just as impressive was the trading of services. I used to watch all kinds of young and old men help out with the hay harvest each summer and watch them pile up cone-shaped hay stacks that in turn were picked up later and heaved twenty feet high onto horse-drawn wagons.

This was a good time for me, as I went out on search and destroy missions. I used to enjoy terminating field mice that sprang litters under these hay stacks. Better still was jumping onto the hay piles stored in the barn. The dust from the hay has not been forgotten. So many scents.

The aroma of bread cooking with sweet corn, and carrots, and cabbage, and steak, and onion, and beaver castors with fried whitefish, or pike, and smoked catfish or sucker. Man! I had the life, son.

The waft of burning wood in the kitchen stove was one I carried forward into your life. The chopping of kindling and maple, or birch, oak, poplar, was a memory kept alive when I had your company, son. Chop or you freeze. Or go hungry. Or dirty. Remember that?

That's how you took out your frustrations in Wiky, son. Slam! Smack! Bang! Chop. Chop until you sweat. I always appreciated your help, son. You were a good worker. A strong one. My love, how I miss you.

So how is it that a child sleepwalks and pees the bed? Regularly. How young was I? I was just a wee one when I found myself crying at the foot of the stairs. I had taken the tumble route down the stairs and woke up at the bottom corner next to the first two steps to the main floor. How come I was there at my grandma's so often? Was I deserted there by my mom and dad? How come? Were they working? I know my Dad was self-employed and boated to Bii-ga-zi-ga-ning during the week and returned home each weekend. But, my mom, as far I knew was a stay at home. If I was the first born, how come I was left in the care of my grandparents and uncles? How come did I not stay with her in Wiky in our own home? Was our home even built? I don't know.

Was this the reason for my tumbles and feeling cold from wet long johns and having to change? How is it that my Uncle Alphie was the one who changed the bedding and my sodden underwear? The funny part is that I do recall feeling bad for messing Uncle Alphie's bed and waking him. I do remember him changing the bedding. I must have been a dreaded handful.

But I never ever recall anyone yelling or giving me heck. They went about their business as if it was normal for a child to behave accordingly, or were very patient as they might have known stuff about my parents. And who would want to relay any issues to a child? Who would want to punish a child? Nothing troubling comes to mind.

Did I already at this very tender age begin to block or shift memories to the back lockers? Again, it's a puzzle.

In retrospect, I know bedwetting and sleep walking are symptoms of some disturbance. In my adolescent years and into my teenage stage, and for sure, later into my adult years, these actions morphed into sexual release. This is why I was always seeking female company.

Ejaculation replaced bed wetting. Hunting girls was my sleep walk. Entering the vagina might have been my way to return to that pink hue of safety and comfort.

But I do remember the terror of hiding from my dad. I remember kneeling and praying with my mother upstairs in Auntie Josephine's second floor. I do remember the feeling of absolute terror from my mom. She was just absolutely terrified. So was I. I too was just so absolutely over and beyond terrified. Here we were praying for safety. We did not want my Dad to find us. I remember my auntie answering the banging on the door.

"She's not here."

The decibel-pounding noise of that knocking and knowing it was my dad kept us paralyzed on our knees. I remember that day. Very clearly.

To this day, son, anything loud will shatter me inside. It will rock me. It was as unnerving then as it is now. The only difference is that I recognized the source of my jumps and had it worked and fixed to the extent possible. Whew! What a jolt, son.

Then there was the time we found ourselves in a safe house in

Toronto of all places. How did we get there? But I do remember my dad talking to my mom there. And I was listening! I was present. I cannot recall the exact words, but I knew he wanted my mom to come home. And I do remember wanting to return home. She did. With us in tow. By this time I had siblings. I forget who and how many, but certainly one or two at the least. I might have been six or eight years old. Maybe. At any rate, we returned home. To more terror.

My dad lied. I am sure he did. Because for the next long and terrifying phase, I was witness to the most terrifying beatings and fear. Regularly.

By this time we were now in our home. And that was the scene of much drinking. Much partying as they might have called it. Each weekend. Every weekend it seemed. It probably was.

And I came to dread Friday nights. I knew to brace myself with each approaching weekend. I was on guard. I was a child. Very tender. I was not yet a man.

One event of many seems to take precedence. I remember I was upstairs. Was I woken up? But I heard the run up the stairs. I knew it was my mom. Since upstairs was divided into two partitions, I first heard and then saw my mother slide under the bed immediately at the top of the stairs. Seconds later, the weight of my dad's footsteps approached. I think he came and searched in the room I was in and quickly turned, just as my mom slid out from under the bed and he then chasing after her. I was rooted to my spot.

He must have caught up to her somewhere outside the house. It was night and it was late. What I heard next but could not see was the most god awful sounds of men jeering and laughing on the road in front of our house. Why were they laughing? Why were they having fun watching my mom beat up? I did not understand this behavior. How come no one was helping mommy? I do not know if I cried. Nor do I remember any siblings present.

This memory blends with another in a similar scenario. I remember my mom being dragged by her hair down those stairs. Upside down. Her head was leading the charge down the stairs. And I remember her pleading.

"Dave. Dave. Please don't."

It seems this horror repeated itself each weekend over some twelve years. And I came to dread each Friday. As fearful as I was before each Friday, Sunday evening brought relief. A yo-yo pattern was the constant. How could they face another in-between?

Leading up to each and every Friday night was the heightened awareness and the wait—the hyper-vigilance. To this day I hate waiting. Waiting is destabilizing. It knocks off my equilibrium. And I do like stability. I do like routine. Routine comes with a certain level of calm.

I dislike chaos. Chaos on the other hand trained me to be alert for danger. Anything that could potentially cause fear and instability. Especially strong was my need to protect.

Thus the martial arts. I developed into a trained neutralizer. I was also good at reconnaissance. Able to look ahead with stealth, gauge, weigh, and set escape routes. It got to the point where I sought control.

Thus my zeal to protect. When you were with me, especially as an infant, and later a toddler, I took my job very, very seriously. At no time was I allowing danger into your periphery. Funny, eh, son? With that one willow whipping, I was the danger. I was the dangerous one. See how warped I was? If the formative years are the first three, I did exactly as memory served. I was my parents. All in one.

They might have quit the drinking and scaring the shit out of their children, but the antics continued. There was my Mom fooling around with my Dad's friend. And then there was my Dad also fooling around with the babysitter. And I saw and heard both.

"Cripes!" as you used to say.

Cripes is right. You got that right. Son, I don't like talking about these things. I don't get off on it. Nor do I blame everyone else for the way I grew up. Like I said, the fault is mine. Not all. But I will take what is mine. I have tried to tell you how and what kind of dad you inherited.

These antics must have pissed me off. I remember taking a red willow stick and whipping you son. My fault. All mine. I apologize for that. But that was the way I was raised. Whipping. In my case it was the belt. In school and at home. I am sorry son. I did not know what I was doing. I acted without thinking. And I was an adult. No excuse. My boy, I did the same with your sister. Oh, the monster I was! Maybe I still am. Just contained is all.

Whatever, I am now aware of this sick behavior. Being aware stopped further beatings.

I do blame the Church and its minions. They taught us violence. I remember the nuns taking out their black straps and flailing away at my hands. What for? I do not remember. But I do remember the lily white hands that disappeared into their black cuffs. They enjoyed whipping. Maybe they were S and M types. Wouldn't surprise me. Assholes! Of the first order.

I do remember my dad taking his belt out on me at some point for reasons I cannot recall. That was painful. And dreaded. And like a proud descendent, I carried that tradition forward. What a prick eh, son? Me. I'm talking about me. I was the prick. Numero Uno. And this is what continued into your childhood. I remember the time. For more drama did I ask you to go and get the red willow from the brush? Shit!

My dad the saint. Just like me. I saw him kissing the babysitter, Mom was away in the hospital having one of my siblings. And there was my dad at the top of the same stairs smooching, kissing, yes, kissing the lady that was our babysitter. Sneaky I was, I had tip-toed up the stairs and peaked through the handrails. I guess I knew something was up.

Then there was my mom making out with my dad's friend downstairs in the same house. It was late. It was dark. And I was maybe six? Seven? Something woke me up.

"Oh, you big bulldozer."

I heard his laughter. I recognized it.

"Mommy. Mommy," I cried.

I actually was crying. I wanted my mom back. I guess I had made enough noise to get her upstairs. She was in her underwear and bra. She did not seem particularly concerned. Whatever she said or did with me must have consoled me enough to put me back to sleep.

Then there was the time her friend stopped at the road in front of our house, and left. My mom went out the front door. And it was not even bed time proper. She left without an explanation.

I knew her friend had brought her brother, for my mom. So they had this ongoing thing for some time.

"I hear you have a girlfriend," asked Mother.

Dad was there. And he denied it. But I sensed it was true. At that time, my dad was working in Sudbury and again was away for the week and returning each weekend.

Great modeling, eh, son? These were my guides. They were my guides for upbringing and getting along with others. It was the how-to for idiots. They taught me how to treat a spouse and what you can expect from a spouse. And, how to treat that spouse. Great. Just great.

I can just hear your sarcasm in your best Mr. Burns voice while making a steeple with your hands, "Excellent." You were so good at that.

Somehow, somewhere, I realized I would not, could not, impart this dysfunction to my children. Ever! I tried. How did I do son?

My Mom died when she was forty-four. And my dad at fifty-seven. You were only an infant when they went home. How are they? Tell Mom miigwetch for her last and only known visit when she answered my question about her condition.

"Well . . ." my mom responded. I awoke with a start.

I only mention Mom's visit because I want you to tell her, had I not been so wound up I might have stayed long enough to enjoy her visit. Tell her miigwetch for guiding us out from chaos and into some lucid understanding of your gift to see visitors and other non-human things from the other side.

When this visit occurred, the family was now stabilized. That means no more drinking and very bad house parties. Weekends were now what I thought they should be: restful.

If my parents quit drinking by the time I reached grade nine, and I had to move away from home and the rez, and into alien life in the city of Sault Ste. Marie, I ask, how old was I? I use this as a gauge. It's approximate. My dad used to pick me up from the greyhound station in Espanola. The best memory of these pick-ups was my dad shaking my hand with a smile as I got off the bus.

My point? It was too late. In retrospect, too much damage had been done. Too little. Too late!

The damage was there. I know. It's a wonder you survived. It's beautiful to see the kind and loving father you turned out to be for the girls and a nurturing big brother for your siblings. I was proud of you. Proud that you were so fussy with detail and not afraid to try something new. Through it all, it's the funny bone and wise cracks you were so quick to deliver. And you spoke your mind. And you were unafraid to show your love for your dad. Thank you. Thank you, son.

Remember the time we went to the summer ceremonies in Garden River? We both got a thanks and appreciation for our way of life. Remember we were standing in front of the sacred fire? Remember your hands were clutched in prayer? You might have been four years old. But you were already in prayer. Who taught you? It was not me. I assume it was someone from home. But I do not see anyone there as being overtly religious. Maybe they were. It's a question I now think about.

It was a Christian gesture commonly seen in the Catholic Church. And I certainly was not of the cloth. My way was the tradition of our people. Fire and spirits. Honor and respect. Thanksgiving and placating. Tobacco and sage. Humility and purification. Sacred Pipe circles. The sacred at the center kept everyone humble and the men and women as equals. The women were the glue. They in turn were the creators that gave direction and provided the serenity to the gathering of pipe carriers and medicine lodge keepers. The elders gave sway.

They in turn were kept in-check by the reminder to stay human and acknowledge and tell one's lessons learned from trials, hardship, and success. No one boasted the amount of cars or the size of their houses or wallets. Most of us, if not everyone, was humbled by the sanctity of life, and how quickly it could change for the worse and even end.

I know you would not remember John. He was one of the lodge keepers and also a student of tradition. He wore his braids long and with pride. He was unhindered by society and brought up his young family in the ancient manner. The precepts of courage, universal love and humility kept this man grounded. Too bad he had to die too soon. And he was younger.

But I remember him standing just to one side and behind

us as we made our path to the fire. I was explaining the purpose of the fire and gathering and our responsibilities as Nishinaabe. I remember him smiling after we were done. You were just a little guy, son. Here you were standing with your tiny hands clasped in prayer.

You were in an azure long sleeve top and elastic waist blue jeans. Your face, hands, and clothes were clean. Your cherubic face listened and gazed into the fire. I cannot remember what I said, but whatever it was brought a smile to John. I noticed him there after we were done.

"You just did a good thing," said John. Then off we went.

That day came back to me when I was trying to recall memories. What did I teach my boy? What good things did I do with my boy? That ceremony under the tall pines of Garden River on a bright sunny day arrived to touch my heart. That day was special. The first ceremony we attended together, son. I was so proud of you.

I like to think this was part of your self-autonomy and standing strong in society's conformity. I like to think this day reinforced your roots with the earth and creation. Did it? Was it? I so much want to think so.

By college it became worrisome when you changed from one stream to another. I know you were unhappy with the rules and demands of study and the conformity of Western-based and designed curriculum. Hotel and hospitality management paid off years later in Lake Louise and ultimately the Yukon and other places I did not know about. Two weeks off and two weeks in a remote fly-in camp seemed to bring contentment. And that is the time you sent me that last email.

Cooking at home was a fussy and fun experience. Was it not, son? I used to howl when you gave me a good talking to; you were so particular.

"Dad. It's gotta look good. You gotta have the right mix of color and food!"

And your steak had to be marinated just so. And it had to be a T-bone, did it not? Otherwise you kept it marinated that much longer.

"Okay, Pops! Dinner is served."

Oh. How I miss those words, son. How I miss your care and attention to detail. And the pride in serving your dad.

"Yah wanna go see a movie, son? The Titanic is playing."

"Nah . . . I know how it ends." Again, the laugh.

Or, the "I'm Bart Simpson. Who the hell are you?"T-shirt that you wore in the streetcar one day during your visit in Toronto? I remember that time. People chuckled as they noticed and pointed at your yellow T-shirt. And you were just a kid. I overheard one chick asking her friend, "Who is Bart Simpson?"

You were ahead of your time, son. I think you were also spoiled. An only child. I don't remember if that was the time you arrived at Toronto International Airport. I was there to meet you. You were coming in from Elliot. I remember waiting outside the arrival area for my little boy. I laughed when I saw you in one of those go carts with a stewardess or somebody official like that driving up the concourse. And there you were all dressed up in jeans, windbreaker and sitting tall beside the young lady. I waved and she pulled over.

"Hi, son! Made it, huh?" I was beaming.

"Is this your father?" she asked.

"Yup! Sure is," and off you were with the cart. What I remember is the mature young child. Unafraid. Confident. And sitting straight up. As if it was customary. Nothing less would do. But, not arrogant. Just sure of one's self.

I suppose that is why you chose to spend your last days in the Yukon. As far away as possible from people. Yet, the life of the party when in a group.

What was that one prank at the hotel? You had the police "Do not enter" yellow tape roping off the reception area? Scared the heck out of them when the crew arrived for their shift. I know there is a lot more to this story. But I remember the laughing when you told me this story. You enjoyed people, but given the opportunity you were gone. Away from them. I know they drained you. No wonder you moved as far as away as possible given the chance. I like that. I would also.

People have a way of taking what they need. Then they forget soon after. Too soon. Then they blame ya for their downturn. Always got to blame someone else. So, yeah, I understood your reasons for moving to the Yukon and then on top of that, cooking at a remote fly-in place. Yup. I understood, son. Not right away. But thinking back, yup. Yes sir.

One part of this decision is medicine people, those that have the ability to see beyond or further into the physical plane, sought lone time and in turn were fed and watered and clothed by the community. This all unraveled with the Euro-centric arrival.

I do not think I prepared you fully for this outlook.

"Grim."

Had my head been on straight I would have taken the time to explain. But no, the idiot I was, and not fully thinking ahead, "Oh, I'll do it next time," never arrived.

But it has, has it not? You went up and died. Here I am scratching my ass and then licking my paws. What a shit, eh, son? Too late. The post-apocalyptic is the wrong time to try and share guidance.

You went up ahead without me, your dad. I think in a true sense, I should have gone ahead to recon and bring back Nanabozho and his manifestations for your guidance and strength to survive in an alien world no longer kind, or, comprehending the Nishinaabe way of looking at life and death and the relationship between both and their influence in everyday physical realm and dream state, as people want to call it. Crap! My fault.

In hindsight you were a teacher and visionary, son. No wonder the state of humanity might have called you a non-conformist.

"Give me your clothes, your boots, and your motorcycle." Remember that? You were so good with Arnie. You sounded just like him. There have been times, I gather, I managed to sound like him also as folks laughed. Imagine that, son. Or, "What the hell?" from the same movie with that black guy lifting the garbage bin.

So in memory of you, I continue to say these lines. Doubt if I sound anything like the original, but at times for a laugh or question, I try.

"Shut up ya dummy!" That was from Redd Fox. I laughed.

Then I would play fight and attack you, grab you by the head, and pretend punch you. Laughing all the way.

"All you'll see are tracers," you used to holler back.

"Yeah right. I'll have you down so fast, son," I joked.

"Yeah sure, Dad." I can still see your beaming face.

Reminds me of the story where this guy was kicking you in the head. He kept kicking you again and again.

"I remember him kicking me over and over," you said. "But I kept my head covered with my hands and arms. I knew he was going to get tired. Sure enough, he quit. Then I got up and proceeded to beat the crap out of him. And he had managed to break his foot over my head." Good plan, son.

I don't condone violence. But whatever happened that night in Elliot, I'm glad you could take care of yourself.

"I jumped into the ditch each time I saw a car coming." This was a good one. Sad but good.

This was the time you escaped from Sagamok and walked home to Cutler. Took you all night but you got home to Gram's by daylight. You were afraid of a posse. Jeez.

But I gotta laugh at this one. It's not funny, but it's a story:

"Move your fat ass!" you said to this woman in a bar.

"What did you say?" said her boyfriend.

"Ya heard me."

Then the fight was on.

"We were so hot. And thirsty. All we wanted was a drink. And this fat ass woman was taking up all the space at the bar. So that's what I said. By the end, they threw out this guy and her girlfriend. And me and Chris laughed and sat down and had our beer."

Son. That's not funny. Yet it is.

7.

KII-NII-ZAAN-ZI-MI
(Dangerous)

"Jaba the Hutt." That's what you used to call me when my belly buried my abs.

I remember your Star Wars collection. You had everything. All the spaceships and all the characters. The little figures and all their names. I forget with who, but I remember you having an animated discussion about who came first or what they did in which scene or episode. Did that movie have sequels?

I seem to remember Yoda and Chewy each having their voice. You should have been a comic on stage.

I truly regret not supporting your dream. You did want to be a comic. And I discouraged and spouted the usual gibberish about pursuing some REAL job and career, and how your studies should be chosen accordingly. Asshole! What a shit I was. Dumb, stupid me.

I still see the drop in your face.

Damn. I still am angry at myself.

What can I say? I fucked up. Royally.

I'm sorry, son. I know it's too late.

It's too late.

This anger had to come from me, son. Sure those fights were victorious. And funny. But at the end of the day, I have had to take stock and ask myself, were you angry? Did I transfer anger to you? What did I do to make you angry? Perhaps the answer is in my own upbringing.

Certainly the bulldozer, kissing babysitters, and a ringside seat at my parent's violence had to have some sort of deep and lasting impression. Those wounds would have been left raw and festering from day one. Whenever that was.

I did not want to be like my dad. I was a festering infection-dripping trauma by the time you came along, son. Sure I woke up at some point, and came to some sort of awareness and resolution. But it was not voluntary. I crashed. I had a breakdown. And I was all of forty or something.

I remember slowly keeling over.

"I'm sick."

The trauma in all its devastation had caught up with me. No longer could I hold back the insecurities, fears, angers, and the pretend jovial self I had presented all my life. It was the picture I showed everyone. You included.

With this onslaught I knew I was in trouble. Then I got scared. And I got angry at the same time. Panic and the need to run to my mommy enveloped me. I began to hyper-ventilate. At the same time I was trying to maintain control. I did not want to go crazy. I felt I could. Then another wave of fear seized me. It was this fear of losing control or dying that was at the forefront. I did not want to die. I did not want to end up in the looney bin.

From this point, my life changed-for the worse. This was the visible beginning of my illness. And I had no idea what was wrong with me. None. All I knew was I was going to go crazy. Or die. And I was petrified.

Sometime before this event I could not sleep. Or from the sleep I had, I would at times jump out of bed and greet the day. Exhausted as I was, I met the day. With a smile.

My thoughts were a hundred miles an hour. It's like that gerbil on the wheel. Running but not getting anywhere. Each day was a struggle to maintain focus and address whatever was in need at home or the task at hand.

I did not think much of this sleep, of this adrenaline rush that began daily. Nor did I think about the nap I had to sneak in once or twice during the waking hours. If I was driving, I pulled over for a quick nap.

The snore or the kick usually I could count on to wake me up. Refreshed. But only for an hour or maybe two. Food had a way of putting me to sleep. Whenever I ate, I tried to plan ahead for a nap. I tried to be strategic.

That snore or kick were the signs of sleep apnea and restless leg syndrome. Just did not know it. It would be years before I was diagnosed. Those were the other issues that kept me from a full night's rest.

I was literally choking myself and starving for oxygen. And the heaving and pulling to breathe kept me working all night when I should have been resting. I could have had a heart attack, son. My organs were functioning at full capacity twenty-four hours a day. The legs and arms lashed out with such force and frequency. I was a shaking, non-breathing mass of taut tissue.

Then the breakdown happened. No wonder I was a basket case by this time. But no one knew. I put on my best acting for years. Even after the event in the clinic. I held on. You would have been proud of me.

Remember the time you came over with Ames and the twins. It was about that time I hit bottom. I still had no idea what was wrong with me. I knew I was not well. But I could go about my business. No one was the wiser.

If you looked at my face from that visit, you could see the lines under my eyes. You would have seen the circles darken my face. My face began to droop. Sure, my smile was there. But inside, I wanted to run. Run away. To where I did not know.

I think this was the only time the girls were in Wiky. They looked so frightened. Yet everyone else was smiles. Son, I am so sorry. For what, I am unsure. But I was a mess. And I am sure I could have been a better grandpa. Love you, son.

I remember the time I took a bead on my grandfather with the twenty-two caliber rifle. It was loaded. Ready for fire. I took careful aim with the front bead centered in the V-notch. I watched as he fussed with fish nets. I remember settling my breathing. My right index finger was on the trigger. The safety was off. He kept fussing with the gear. For some time I stood on the lake gravel not more than sixty feet away, and had the rifle cradled firm. I knew how to shoot. After all, I was and had been part of the dog hit squad.

Our job as kids was to get rid of the litters that appeared once in a while. My cousins and I were good at it. We usually would prop them up on a post or pole of some sort, and make sure there was nothing but bush behind the critter, and then we would practice our marksmanship. That's just the way it was, son.

So why did I point that rifle? No one knows. I don't. It's a question that remains unanswered.

Grandpa never knew how close he was to death.

Can you see why I never wanted you to be like me? Maybe that was why I kept my distance? Maybe? I don't know.

I do know I did not want to expose my children to violence. I did not want my children to be angry and fearful. I did not want them in paralysis. I wanted to stop the cycle of violence. Stop the wheel. Regain the hoop of health and function.

Did I succeed? At least with some parts, I think.

∽

This is our story. It's ours. It's not meant to be a self-help story. Our story is meant to describe a healing process. The story is incomplete. But it's a beginning.

At the center is the spirituality. Not religion. But done right, it can be religious. Ours is areligious. Ours is the fire, tobacco, steak, muffins, juice and prayer. The center of the prayer is thanksgiving. The thanksgiving is the acceptance of life and death. The light and dark is the heartbeat of the universe. The heartbeat is the pulse and tradition of our people. For millennia the ebb and flow of birth to birth is a stark reminder of our mortality. This mortality keeps us in check. The love and forgiveness adds to our resilience. Knocked down, we gather ourselves, and with all the strength we can muster, take a step, one day at a time. One moment at a time.

There are times when we don't know where we are or where the next step should be heading.

Breathe. When breathing has stopped, the physical will send a reminder. When the emotional is seized, breathing will tell us we are still in agony. The mental can drive us insane. Questions without acceptable answers will have us running the proverbial wheel and not getting anywhere. We will not get anywhere. The fire of the spirit will mercilessly push and drag our existence into a seemingly endless cycle of agony. Agony so deep and all encompassing, and so very methodical in its relentless attack into every fiber and molecule that we wish we were dead.

This same fire of cleansing burns the carnage away for our survival. The deadwood is gone. Burned into ash. Ash in turn seeds our growth. Into this fertile ground, we bury our sorrow, and our pain, and our tears. From this acknowledgement, we define our tomorrow, our next breath. We believe. Hope is useless. Action is belief. Acceptance of the next plane of life is something to desire and work towards.

We accept our temporary existence on this one plane. Belief is the acceptance, we too will get there when the moment arrives. The wheel of life will continue to churn until we step out onto another spoke, which will take us by the hand and lead us into bliss. No more pain. No more sorrow. Only happiness.

8.

GE-ZI-BIN-SHIN
(Preparation)

Gently I wrapped the red bandana on the two-foot high fir tree crown. The tree crown was now your head. Gently I circled the flash around your head. I pulled the two ends tight so it would not unravel. I wanted the bandana just the way you liked it. Firmly, I pulled it up then down and just an inch or so up. Satisfied it looked cool just as you liked your bandana, I stepped back making sure it was just so. I had the knot towards the east and with the front facing west. I wanted you to face home looking good. Satisfied the bandana would not drop, I again adjusted the strip and made sure the two ends graced your back. Now it was ready.

This six foot length of red cloth symbolized your headdress of bright red feathers that you wore on your visit. It was also in honor of Papase.

With this part of the ceremony of the dead complete, I again stepped back and circled your grave.

Earlier I had prepared a grave for your internment. The hole in the ground had been lined with semaa, ash from the fire, and fine soil sifted from the gravel. I wanted you to prosper. And I wanted you to be comfortable. Snug. Warm. And ensure your presence was clearly marked and noticeable.

Earlier, Angie and I placed your remains into the ground. She dropped tears into the hole to keep you hydrated. I was too numb. So I did the next best thing and brought a pail of water. I too, wanted you to be comfortable.

When we had gently placed the ashes into the gravel, a gentle gust of wind smiled on us. The sun was also sending his warmth. Birds were singing and chirping in the trees. Even the flies and mosquitoes seemed to stay back and bow their heads in respect.

"Miigwetch, ngwis. Miigwetch, my boy. I love you."

Behold! You were a sight.

A ring of white stone circled your grave. These stones of

various sizes came from the hole I had dug. The teaching is to put back anything from where it came. They were nice oval white rocks that encircled your permanent home on earth. With earth as the anchor, I added spokes to emanate outward from the grave. Each was for a cardinal direction. I began with the west and then north as these were your power points. From here I again gathered appropriate sizes to serve as posts for each doorway. Two rocks framed each direction. I stepped back to study.

The hoop was complete. The wheel was now visible. The medicine semaa was placed on top of each stone. It was now the sacred. The semaa came from a small pouch that held a picture of your smiling face. This came from your mother. Not wanting the pouch to fly away, I placed another stone on top of the northern gateway rock on which it sat.

This semaa was for offerings and special requests.

The circle was big enough to accommodate entry and exit. One could walk the circumference of the grave comfortably and visit each direction. One could enter from any direction, according to their needs.

Spokes emanated outwards from the grave. Each spoke was designed from the smaller stones specially selected for their size from the stone pile I had earlier gathered from the gravel and stone of the grave. From this same pile came the larger stones. Two were selected for each direction. And I kept adjusting them to ensure an adult could comfortably enter and exit the wheel of life and death. I seemed to make my doorways too narrow. Adjusted wider to accommodate my girth as a guide, I adjusted each stone to not only serve their practical purpose but also to face the four directions.

For reference I used the setting sun to catch the correct alignment. I remember standing there and watching the tree shadows move with the sun. With one tree serving as a straight line and alignment, I adjusted the eastern doorway stones to sit directly opposite the west. I also took a straight sapling from the fire site to guarantee straightness from a stone in the west to correspond with its twin in the east.

The medicine wheel was now complete. At its center stood the fir tree that Jeffery Geniesse had mailed from Michigan.

The tree was now you. The ash was now your anchor. The spokes were for the rays of life. The stone outcrop symbolized the gateways. The outer circle was for the never ending life and death that stood for our birth and mortality. One could not be complete or exist without the other.

On that tree shone a glistening oval plate with your name engraved. "Shannon Kenneth Cecil Meawasige." And immediately below it, "Papase." This plate came with the tree.

Jeffery, the kind heart he is, shipped the tree whole from Michigan. To my knowledge, no one has ever done this in Wiky. Marking a grave with a blue fir. This little guy stood between three and four feet in height. The red bandana graced the tree's crown. At the same time, it clung to the earth of its people as its length lay under the foot of this young sapling as it was so long. It was as if the tree and sky were attached by an umbilical cord.

Jeffery is a white dude that came across my radar not too long before your untimely demise. We had first met when he was pitching a television pilot with Dad as part of the primary focus. He even shot a couple of segments. One with a smudge ceremony and the other an interview.

Jeffery, a professional videographer with his own company, has a lot of good work and credits. He meant well and it came from a good place. The pitch did not get anywhere. Not surprised, I had told him no one was interested in Native America. History is proof of that. Five-hundred years of genocide is not a comfortable topic America wants to be reminded of. Residential or boarding homes legislated by federal governments and all mainstream churches in Canada and the United States were willing partners in the mass extermination of Indians. That is where "Kill the Indian, and save the man" originated. Their job through biological warfare with smallpox, and continental theft through treaties was not something America was willing to hear. Instead they are happy with the false and first Thanksgiving stereotype imagery.

No one wants to hear about the largest mass hanging of Indians ordered by Abraham Lincoln. Or Benjamin Franklin stating they should copy the freedom and ways of Indians as the basis for free will and equality in their constitution. Nope. Not comfortable at all with any of this.

Odd. America does not know about its history and origins. It's recorded. By them. It's all public.

Blessings to Jeffery.

9.

BAA-BID-ZAN
(HUMOR)

Nanabozho taught us about life, death and everything else in between, after and before birth and death.

One time Nanabozho woke up from a slumber. He scratched his balls and farted. Hungry as always, he stretched, yawned once more, and farted one more time. Whew!

"What dat mell?" Nanabozho was known to speak funny at times.

"I said, wat dat smell?"

No one answered. "Hmm"

"Aaniish naa iidik?" he asked.

"Minjiidik" came the voice.

"Who said dat?" Nanabozho replied.

"Niin." Came the reply.

Nanabozho jumped from his bunk, hit his head on the top bunk shelf, yelled, "Ouch!" and landed with a thud on the floor.

"Cripes. My arthritis," he yelled.

"Shut up dummy," came another reply.

Annoyed at the trickery, Nanabozho launched into a three-sixty. He dropped-kicked as he swung his tail with the speed of a dervish. Realizing he hit nothing, as nothing was there to hit, Nanabozho was now more annoyed than ever.

"Brother Nanabozho,"

"What?" answered Nanabozho, even more annoyed now.

"Brother Nanabozho."

"WHAT?" yelled Nanabozho.

"I said what. Who is this? Where are you? Come and show yourself," demanded Nanabozho, now pissed off more than ever.

Nanabozho could feel his brown crunch and furrow. He farted again, this time with a gusto. "Take that you idiot."

"Whew. Dat smell," he thought to himself. Even Nanabozho, at times, couldn't stand the smell of his cloud. Especially if he was downwind. Even worse was when he was snuggled under the down blankets during the coldest of winter nights.

One time he dreamt he was in the most foul of dark secrets somewhere deep under this world. And it stunk. Everywhere he looked there were walking farts trying to escape the winds. And some of them, he knew. So he thought. But he was unsure. He would have stayed longer but a blast of foul air blew him against the wall of plume, bounced off, and mercifully somehow found a means of escape into goose down falling out from the deer hides that he had stolen from some geese some time ago.

Relieved it was only a dream, Nanabozho stuck his snout out and pulled in a great whiff of ice crystals.

For a moment this is what this foul air reminded him of. Secretly, he did enjoy the occasional smell of his air. Some farts were quite pleasant. He inhaled them when they did happen to come along, which was once a while, but not always.

"Okay, where are you, dude?" he inquired again. "Show yourself," he demanded.

"Nope. Not I. Not now. Not today," came the response.

"How come?" Nanabozho was now curious. And how come you smell like that?" he added.

"Oh, you have no idea," came the reply.

"Yikes," thought Nanabozho.

Just to be sure it was not his rear he smelled, he craned his neck and torso around, back, and down and took a good whiff of his fart hole. Sometimes, dung would get caught on his fur and have that funny odor that repelled some of his friends away. "What?" he would ask.

With muffled laughter, and squeaks, and chirps, the squirrels, birds, and rabbits jumped away to holler out loud away from Nanabozho. Even the Skunk would roll on the ground in laughter, pissing and farting away as he rolled onto his long tail, which, he too, took in the occasional fragrance. With a grin.

"If you do not treat your brothers and sister well, if you do not treat them with respect, if you do not feed them, if you do not dry their tears, if you do not sit with them when they have lost someone close to them, especially one of their young ones, Nanabozho—"it called him by name, Nanabozho realized, and a wash of guilt swept over him as he adjusted his tail, ears, and washed his face from the trout stream below his feet, where his summer home was located.

"You, Nanabozho, is destined for life without friends. But, even worse," continued the voice, "you will never ever again enjoy the smell of your fart, because you will be forced to hold in your fart until you are ready to explode."

"Yipes," thought Nanabozho to himself.

Immediately he recalled the time he ate too many crab apples. And chose to not share any. Not even with the brother crab apple tree nearby. And when these apple trees wilted, crusted over, and went to permanent sleep, he did not give it a second thought as he went prancing away to look for something else to eat.

"Me first," was his favorite saying. He marveled at his own success, His bounty was next to none.

Forced to rethink his ways, Nanabozho, shrugged his shoulders, wagged his tail, licked his scrotum, bit off a bug from his testicles, jumped up, and turned three-sixty. Satisfied he was in a trance or sleepwalking, and it was all his imagination, Nanabozho blurted a fart and pranced away. A wet trickle ran down his ass hairs. The entire forest throng chuckled and marveled at Nanabozho's ability to survive his own cloud.

With a start Nanabozho stood on all four legs, shook his head, neck, and torso and stopped when he heard the calls from the deep.

"Brothers, Sisters, where are you?"

Once he oriented himself, he bounced away in search of ducks. They were good to eat. And off towards the setting sun he skipped. Then Nanabozho was gone.

ဢ

If anything should be communicated, the comfort zone for death and good deeds needs support. Death as an uncomfortable topic and a way of life is best kept in the open. Unlike Nanabozho, the need for community and sharing should be brought out from fear and into acceptance, and to help others.

In our case we had some tools that eased the transition. However abrupt and mind-numbing your demise, the families had anchors in the traditions of our peoples.

Your mother asked me to take the lead with the preparations. What could I say? One, I was the father.

Had our death people been available as the recognized group to lead, instruct and guide the families left behind, I would have been confident. Since these groups no longer existed, it was up to us and the families to wing it, and reach for anything culturally available. Thus the cleansings, eagle feather, drums and songs. I think this tiny morsel of cultural ownership paved the way out from a very dark moment.

In the old days, each and every individual in the group was prepared for crossing over and openly discussed the day of his or her demise. Death discussion was a topic not to be ignored or to fear. Death was a part of life. So when your mother asked that I take the lead, I answered and without pause, in the affirmative. My job was to oversee general cultural protocols.

I had some two hundred dollars to bring you home and pay for the funeral. I was broke. So, I decided to file for bankruptcy. I saw no other way. Surprisingly, most creditors took it quite well and were willing to wait. My landlord agreed to cancel my lease due in August and use my deposit to cover the last month's rent. That was a huge relief. Special thanks to Pat, owner of Turtle View Apartments.

There was no way my last paycheck could cover living and funeral costs. Most offered their condolences and were willing to work towards a solution. I delayed the bankruptcy.

This meant I could keep both cars and the insurance for the vehicles. For a bit. In my sick head, I was willing to walk to work. No problem, I thought. This way I could lose the two hundred and thirteen pounds of ugly fat I had accumulated over the years.

"Jaba the Hutt," you used to call me when my six pack disappeared over the years.

I had been told I carry it well, but my short five-foot-six frame still looks like a fat dwarf.

Which reminds me. Did I ever tell you the story about lil' green men? Well, not actually green men, but small, yes.

It was during grade seven or eight when I inadvertently let out the story about the little people during wood working class. Mr. Pugh was going on about this and that shave or cut on the band saw. I must have felt quite comfortable when I blurted out that my grandfather was in the habit of talking to the little people.

"What's your Grandpa drinking?" he quipped, the ass ol'.

It was at that time I realized that white people have absolutely no awareness of those worlds familiar to our culture. I know you laughed when you came across these types of experiences. That old ugly white guy taught me and the rest of the class, a class of my peers, that they would dismiss anything considered fairy tale, and anything which could not be probed, measured, counted, inhaled or drunk. Which is fine. I know we had no problem with Western science. But me and you grasped for and lived in at least two worlds.

In high school I had a twenty-eight inch waistline. Now it is a gross thirty-eight. And even that stretches to the outer limits.

"You're just getting old, Dad."

True. Too much car business I guess.

"Come on, Dad. Step on it. Even the white-haired old people are passing us," used to be a good laugh. It was true. Old white hairs used to pass us on the highways. And all I was doing was following the speed limit and keeping safety first.

Walking has been my way to keep some finesse. Mostly in the woods and away from folks. In the city, it's hard to do with so many white people everywhere. Remember the time I told you about the little old white ladies clutching their purses closer and tighter when I happened to meet them on the street. We laughed didn't we, son?

Imagine that. White people are still scared of Indians. White people are scared of everything. They are never alone. And they are always yacking. Non-stop. Even in the woods. Not only are they scared of their shadows, they are petrified of weeds in their yards. Heavens! What a plight. They control their own gardens as they try to search to control the woods and forests that once graced the continent. Those dark forests might hide a creeping Indian. Funny folk, eh, son?

There was a time I used to run for miles. Discovered this some time back. Finally learned that my spine was wacked out of shape. Just worn out, I guess. Chiropractors sent their kids to college and paid for material things from my payments.

Fuck the bankruptcy, son. Fuck the material. What hurts the most is the loss of your company. This was the true bankruptcy. The loss of your company. Those happenings that shed light into my daily life. The tradition of sharing jokes and laughter together and making fun of each other. This was our love. Indian style.

There was one time I never told you about. This was the time you were drunk at the casino. Your friend and coworker from the casino had to escort you home. I was scared then. Not that you made any gestures to warrant my fears, but that was just the way I was wired. Violence scared me. It came from watching my dad beat up my mom for so many years.

I hid my fear of men. I also hid my fear of loud voices. Men's only. It was decades before I could crawl from this pit. But even now, I quake a bit on the inside when I hear men, especially if they are drinking.

It was in Timmins that I discovered the martial arts. This was my way to protect you, sonny boy. It was also my way to make you strong. It was also my way to conquer my fears and not pass them on to you. It also became a survival skill.

I think I had visions of teaching my boy one day. Sadly, that never happened. My fault.

During high school I used to draw these flying Karate kickers that I saw in these magazines I used to purchase. It would not be a decade later that I would actually begin to study the rudiments of genuine hard-core no fancy-flowery self-defense. This was back when I could do push-ups on my thumbs, three fingers, or back wrists, which, up until your demise, I could show off when asked. This ended with your demise. But give me time, I'll return.

Later when I taught my own classes I had to show the students. Kids. Young adults. I suppose they were all frightened of smashing their wrists. Not that I blame them. Most kids come with weakened constitutions.

Thanks to my instructor, Sensei Don Girard, who taught me to put anyone down on the street or in the dojo. And I was not a bigger guy then. In class, most of my men students were larger and taller than me. At least one was over six feet. And they were not wimps either. They were Indian. All of them. They are still around today. Tough mothers.

I am sure they remember the pain. Wado-ryu is an ancient

martial art that does not mess around. It gets the job done with devastation.

Remember Don, son? He was there in Timmins when we lived there. I have not even told him of your death. He does not know. The last time I tried contacting him, I discovered his number was disconnected. I am hoping he comes to the Pow-Wow as he has done over the years.

Don taught me much, son. One of the things he taught is a skill he patented and shared with me on our last visit. It is this exercise that has kept me going. Slowly. Ever so gently. Because I have had the shit kicked out of me, unlike any punch or kick encountered in all my years of training. It is a simple repetition that I have tried to apply daily. It's been hit or miss.

It's an exercise that kicks out my demons. It is also a way to release the loneliness. Even if it's just a few minutes. Before you went home, I could do this exercise with great stamina. Gentle, yet, strengthening. My spine kept supple and fluid. At one point I was up to one-and one-half hours. Talk about a powerful tool that kept me alive and breathing. Best of all, it has kept me totality in the moment and gave me strength of mind to focus and not go insane. The incredible energy created allows me to tap into the same universal power the Nishinaabe are familiar with. That practice has kept me going. Say a word for our friend and teacher, Sensei Donald Girard, won't you, son? Please.

With the battle for survival and to bring you home, family generosity arrived, and we were able to meet with the undertaker and make the final arrangements. Yup. My two-hundred or so measly dollars were thrown into the kitty. If I could have, I would have paid for the whole darn thing. Fuck the money. It's only money. Can't take it with you. Right, son?

The bill came to some ten-thousand dollars.

Self-care. Indian style. Without the care of material or zhooni'yaa. This is the way I taught you, son. You were a good student, son. You passed with flying colors. As for me, I am royally pissed off all the time. The images in my mind all have to do with defense and developing ideas for victory over anyone. Usually with a person. I am alert. Yet I yawn. I am in a stupor. It's all in my head. I do not have the energy to act. Even wiping myself is a chore.

"Too much information, Dad."

Yeah. I know. But I cannot seem to find the source of this anger. I just cannot fathom it. I do realize it has to do with your dying and leaving. But exactly how? To which point of the equation is the source of my angers. I do not know.

One thing I do know is that I was pissed-off at myself for not having the means to bring you home. If it were not for family, you'd be stuck out there.

My torso aches. My stomach aches. My chest feels empty. A nothingness filled my chest. A never-ending onslaught. Weary. Limp, I droop. Stooped.

I also know I am not angry at you. Nada. Zip.

I am however angry with the world. Why? For not stopping. The entire world should stop whatever they are doing and pay heed and respect for my son who has died. No one gives a shit. The world doesn't give a shit. They just don't.

It reminds me of the time my dad died. I was so angry! Why didn't people stop what they were doing and pay attention? I recognize that same anger. Again, I was not mad at my dad. Just mad at the world. This anger seems bent on destroying me from the inside out and no one knows about it. I keep it all to myself.

I wouldn't even know where to begin.

As sick and pissed-off an angry shit I was, I knew I had to do something. Through pissed off vapors clumped between my eyeballs and cerebral cortex, I somehow found the energy to gather one herb from my yard.

This plant was the first remedy taught by my grandmother.

"Do this, and you will have a long life," she said, as she handed over a branch on our walk home back to the farmhouse. I must have been six or seven. Maybe eight years old. Tops. It tasted not unpleasant.

Since then I have used it a hundred times and instructed others on its applications. Because it works in many ways, grief and anger were the targets to remedy. From the top of my white hairs to my twisted toenails, and a seeping cauldron of pain from somewhere deep within, I prepared the mixture. My soul was dying.

Plants are people. They listen and go to work as soon as we ask them for help. They do whatever it is they can do. I placed semaa down as an offering and thanksgiving. It was also an apology for breaking off a limb.

"Forgive me. And help me. I need your help," is a common cry for treatment.

I treated myself. Alone. When done, I returned the remains outdoors, back on the ground. I was still angry, except the pain was not so acute. I returned to my comatose position and laid there numb and way beyond exhausted.

I apologize for not teaching you more of our herbs and their applications. None of these are available in any herb book. Sure, aspirin is derived from the willow, but the spirit of that willow and its cousins goes way beyond aspirin. The spirit of that plant is the reality. Like I said, the spirit of any plant is the real physician.

If we are in tune and give the proper protocol and respect and honor, then the plant will tell us which part of its anatomy to use. It is either the root, bark, leaf, picked at the proper time of the sun, moon, and season that helps. One must know the seemingly infinite details for each plant. Its age is important. And many more details best kept between teacher and student. That is the way of our traditions.

You did fine, son. The respect and humility were grasped. So proud of you.

In return I ask you to help me live and find the means to help myself. For I am so tired, son. I am so tired from being tired. I'm tired of crying. I'm tired of feeling heavy and pissed-off. I am tired of crying. Will it ever stop? Will I ever be happy again?

I never knew I was so happy until you died, son. I ceased to smile and be happy on that day.

10.

ZHAM-SHIN
(DINE)

True to our culture, I cannot recall if I was ever alone after your death.

From my earliest days, I remember food, quiet conversations, with the occasional and very loud outburst of a laugh, then muzzled laughs at a wake. The custom is to not leave someone alone, usually the spouse, significant other, or the parent or children.

From the moment news arrives of one's death, people would always ask, "Well, is there somebody there, now?"

The idea behind that question was to ensure the bereaved was not alone and had company. This goes back to the hoop idea all are interconnected through this great cycle. Each person may not necessarily know the other, but will acknowledge the frailty of life and how it can change in a moment.

"At any time," is what the people say.

Nothing is taken for granted. Nothing is controlled.

And perhaps this was my greatest strife. The realization that life is free from control, independent, and cannot be controlled. It was and is out of my hands. My boy's life, my dear Papase, had his own life line independent of any control from the protector, father, teacher, and no way could I control one iota of death's swoop.

I used to pride myself in knowing my children never went hungry, were protected from any harm, clothed in sensible attire for the season, and married to the idea of later. I would see you later. I would talk to you later. I will tell you next time. What an arrogant ass. Dumb. And stupid on top of that.

Now it's too late. Here I am composing my thoughts on paper for you to hear. What good is it, eh, son? Too little. Too late again. Am I fooling myself? Is this writing a foolish exercise? What purpose will it serve? Anything? Nothing?

Is it my guilt? Yes. I think so. For being a shit face! I am so sorry, my son. Forgive me. I just have to keep writing. Maybe I'll join you when I am done writing. Who knows? No one does. Maybe I'll drop before I get to the next page. I don't know. I know shit, son.

All I know is nothing. This stuff can fit in an acorn shell. That is the amount of life I know. Death? Very little.

"How long have you been crying?" nephew asked.

"Two months" I replied.

"Oh. That's not long." Came the reply.

It was at that moment that I realized others did not know shit. Especially in the loss of a child. And perhaps that episode, and the big one, got me to write with the pen I never received, and as an exercise, write for the sake of writing and forget about it.

§

The one thing I do know that can be part of that acorn bundle is the closeness of human contact. When I was in the Soo, Cathy and her daughters and our twins kept me alive. A roof over my head, plenty of food, delivered, and a bed and couch to keep myself together. They were the first who acted with love and compassion. It was the most miserable week in my life at that point. Miserable from heartbreak, fear, anger, and anxiety. I kept it to myself.

It was enough to not interact. No one said, "Come on Kenn," do this or that. Or worse, "Be happy." Blah, blah, blah.

For this I was grateful.

Uncle Martin arrived one afternoon dressed in his best slacks, shirt and boots.

"It's to show respect" he replied when Cathy and the others joked with him regarding his attire. His long hair was combed and nicely tucked back. Even when he wanted to leave, I asked him, "Please stay."

"Okay," he nodded.

He had been there several hours and possibly thought his presence was trying by that point, as I was not conversing with him much. But I felt good my dear Martin was there with me and I was not left alone.

The phone calls with Uncle Dennis in Cutler kept us in the loop. He was the point person. He told us to not call your mom as this would cause confusion in an already tense and heart-wrenching time. That was cool. Someone taking charge. And all accepting the suggestion.

I think the Canada Border and Customs agent was also sympathetic. Who would joke about such a thing?

"The reason for your visit?"

"My son died. I'm coming home to bury my son."

I was at home in Wiky after Cutler. Your Mom had gone back to the Yukon with your ashes. Everyone dispersed. I was a mess. I was sad. I was crying. Almost non-stop and without notice. I was an absolute mess. A total basket case.

When I did crawl out of bed, and if I did have shower, and if I did have morning coffee, or ate, I went back and forth between the bed and the couch.

I guess it was no more than two days I was home when company began arriving. I cannot remember who came first. Not that there were many visitors. But the ones I do remember were Eric and Rita. An elderly couple stepped in.

"Biindegek."

With all the might I could muster, I struggled to stay upright sitting on the couch acknowledging their respect.

"Look. Here is a little something," Eric spoke as he handed me one stick of sage. Just one. And for that gesture, it was priceless. First, because they were elders.

I do not recall any other elder couple before them. Eric and Rita stayed for a bit. Then left. It was the effort and the time to visit someone in pain. Me.

Eric has gone home now, son. Have you two met? What did you laugh about?

What did you sing? He was a fun character. You two would have much in common. I can see the two of you together having the time of your lives.

∽

My friend Terry had come in to sit and visit.

"Why are you ever playing such sad music?" Terry asked.

"Because I am sad," I replied with hidden anger.

We had grown up together. Every chance he had, he was at my place. Just the way we were when we were children. One time, we were caught making a fire out in the thicket of willow on the other side of the road and across this main road where we used to play. We used to play with lil' plastic soldiers and blow them up with firecrackers.

"Let's get this pill box."

"Okay."

We then ran for cover and eagerly watched the wick burn towards the eventual explosion.

One time we were sitting out in the back lawn and Terry was munching away on some day old fry bread rolls he had purchased for a dollar each from Eugene. Anyway, we were sitting out there facing the rear of the house. I was in my lawn chair.

Getting a little thirsty or hungry we went into the house. Got whatever we needed and came back out.

"Hey!! Look at those crows," I yelled.

"Where?" Terry asked, looking around.

"Shtaa haa!" he shouted.

And off he went. Out the back screen door, down the three steps of the porch, and off he went like a kingfisher. His short chubby old legs were moving as fast as they could carry a sixty-something-year-old man towards his prized possessions.

"Hyaaah," he shouted as he waved his arms. From inside, I watched him run as fast as an old dog can only muster.

I was laughing. Out loud. Not only was I grinning cheek to cheek, but chuckling something fierce as I took in the backyard scenario. The drama! I could see the four crows look up and look up at Terry. Ignoring him for the moment, they went back to poking the white plastic bag and digging at the contents. His fry bread. But, not only that, his polyester pants were slipping down with every jaunt of his legs. And his underwear was starting to show. I laughed and ran after him.

I caught up to him at the scene of the crime.

"Will you look at this?!" he said in disbelief.

Yup. The plastic bag had been poked through by the crows. There were four. With some sadness, he picked up the bag and loosened the knot. Shaking his head he examined the contents.

Sure enough, each fry bread piece had a hole. It seemed the crows had a taste of each and every one of the four fry bread pieces. They were fussy. They were choosy. Each piece had a gouge from which they tasted the wares. I guess they would have kept dining had we not come out.

"Oh, never mind," he grieved. "They're still good."

With that he resealed the bag and sat down. He was now careful to place the bag firmly within eye view and under his seat.

"Let's see them try now," he said to himself.

To this day, Terry will not leave a bag unattended.

"They are still good to eat," he grinned as he tested one greasy piece. "And I'm taking them home, too."

∾

My friend Irvin placed his huge paw on top of my hand. As usual, I was immobilized in the same spot. My right hand was on the end piece of the leather couch.

"Here. I bring you this," he said gently. I tilted my head up from my chest and looked at his gift of cigarettes.

"Miigwetch. 'Chi-Miigwetch."

I cannot recall how long he stayed. But like Eric and Rita, it was for a bit. And I cannot recall if he said something else. I think he did. But I do remember his touch. The lay of his hand on mine. It was warm. Soft. And nurturing, I suppose. I think he said, something like, "What you are going through is very difficult."

In that moment and in that voice, someone else was recognizing the pain. Someone else was acknowledging your departure. And in doing so, they were acknowledging the total weight and the emptiness of loss. Irvin a gentle giant. He is a big man. He owns his own shop. And he is a good worker. He was one of the ones to show off his garden.

"Ngowa-kaanes," he joked at the time. Like a little graveyard. And that was years ago.

You know what else, son? Each time Angie would go to his store, Irvin would give her a pack or two of smokes.

"This is for your dad," he would say.

Or, "Tell your dad to drop in sometime."

All I could do was nod. To this day, I have not returned to visit. I just do not have the energy to chat. It takes too much out of me. Thus my hermitage, I guess. I shun people. I do not go out anywhere.

Anyway, the teaching is to not go or do something for at least twelve moons after a loss.

"You need wood?" Or "What do you need?" 'Chi-Brian asks.

One time he brought over a home-made cedar two seat gift. He pulled in reverse to the yard and off came a brand spanking new chair. It had a tray between the seats for coffee, snacks or whatever.

"That's for you."

Except for the coffee table sectional in the middle, it was a very solid love seat type.

"Ya just gotta paint," he boasted.

"Okay." But it was angled too far to the rear leaving the short legged host to dangle his feet. Mistake. Back on to the pickup he hoisted.

"Wait. I'll fix it," he said. Not an hour later he returned. Back on the lawn it went. It was perfect. No one has ever given a gift like that. And there it sits. Facing the fire site.

For the sacred fire he brings hardwood maple and oak. And the kindling to go with it. It's all precut and ready for my mallet and axe. It gives me an opportunity to exercise outdoors. One cord at a time. Again, as a gift. He will not take anything in return save for tobacco.

∽

"How are you, Uncle?"

"Sad. My son just died."

"Oh." That brought the conversation to an abrupt end.

This was about the same time I dropped in on some family in the Soo. Must have been a month later. No one said boo. No one gave me a hug. No one asked how I was holding up. Everyone was going about their business, washing dishes, and cooking, and flurrying about this or that. Is that normal? Not to give your own blood a hug? Not even a hello.

Pretty sad, eh, son?

I went and found a couch seat and sat down. No one asked or commented about Shantu or offered a funny story. That hurt the most. How can one go on and not inquire about the journey or not offer some sort of memory in your name. No one did. The only reason I lingered was that our girls were expecting a visit from "Smelly Grandpa," a joke, or prompt to elicit self-deprecating humor.

I envision myself a smelly ol' mess, son. To this day, the girls write Smelly Grandpa when they send email or we have a chance to visit. In fact, I encourage the name.

"Whew. Doesn't Grandpa smell?" I occasionally colored my greetings and hugs, or email. Just a joke. Trying to brighten up one's moment.

And that was your way, son. Ya came up with the one-liners or detailed a story. I knew the audience was enthralled. Like the time you ripped your face open from a ski tumble. I never did see it. Nor did I see any scars from it at the wake. I looked. You must have healed up well. Or the time you cracked open your arm, again from a tumble. Jeez, son. You liked to get a reaction did you not? I vividly do recall the body locaters that you wore down the back when skiing in the avalanche-prone slopes. I knew you were solic-iting a response only to see our reaction. Son, son, son.

It's been twelve painful moons since your departure. My face still drops saliva from the corner of my mouth. Unknown to me. Unknown for some time until I touch my cheek or mouth for a smoke or for food. And I am pretty sure my mouth droops open most of the time.

I wake at about four. As my cousin once said jokingly, "I get up so early, I go about waking the birds."

Well, nothing that energetic. I wake. And that is it. I do not have the ability to do anything else. Not even shower. Sometimes. I choke. I catch myself when I try to grasp a breath. I forget to breathe. Literally. And that gasping scares the shit out of me. My body goes into panic.

I cry incessantly and out of the blue. Just no warning. Maybe just a thought. I have not been invited anywhere, lest I make a scene. Which is okay and understandable. Not only must I smell and stink, and look unkempt, but my whole demeanor must be one of distance, or distanced. I am sure people can see or sense I am withdrawn. And I do not care one bit about their daily bullshit. Nothing. I do not care. I do not care what goes on in the world nor in anyone's lives. It's all petty. I am not there. I am elsewhere. I am with you.

I do react when I hear of someone's misfortune. Especially when someone close dies. Especially if it's their child. This gets me. This gets my undivided attention. But I do not have the strength to say or act. So many people have gone home after you left. I cannot recall the numbers. And that is only in Wiky. Normally, I would have entertained the thought about visitation. In the end, I probably would not have gone. I am burned out from wakes, funerals, and tears from those undergoing extremely hard times.

I did go to one wake on funeral day. I arrived early enough to meet up with the younger brother of the deceased. His old brother used to drop in. This one time I had the courage and strength to prod myself there.

Inside the hall was a dog. It belonged to the deceased. Brownie. The dog had his two front legs on the kneel thingy usually placed in front of the coffin. It was a closed coffin.

"Brownie has been like that every day since they brought the body," my friend explained. "He goes up to the casket and waits as if he wants his master to get out of there and play with him."

Sure enough, Brownie, the large dog, he was straining to look into the casket. His nose and snout were trained over the side of the box. He knew his master was in there. And I do know Brownie knew his master was not returning. He was gone. But he kept vigil.

His doggie tracks led back and forth the front entrance of the hall. He came and went as he wished. His footprints trailed from the outdoors and back to the casket. No one minded Brownie's tracks on the red velvet dais available for kneeling. And no one removed him. Brownie was very calm.

I continue with the anger mode. I am not mad at God or with the death of my first born.

"Maano," as we say.

It goes to show the finality of a breath and its speed to

disappear without warning. Perhaps it's best that way. But like the Indians of old, "Any day, or this day is a good day to die."

Thus the acceptance of death. And the pain of it for those left behind. The deceased has gone on to other places. And that is acceptable. It's not our way to question. Perhaps, all we are left with to question is, did we do right by that life?

Son, I broke the cycle of violence against women and children. In my life. In my way. I cannot control others. But maybe we can. If we tell our story, maybe, just maybe, someone will learn something from it and not act like their Mom or Dad. I have not been totally successful, but I have taken it to the limit. I tell your sisters to defend and stand up for themselves.

I even taught them to defend themselves. One time your sister was grabbed by the arms in the school yard. Typical of a bully, he held your sister's hands against the wall. Not one day earlier, we had gone over this scenario. If this happens, this is what you do, I instructed. Smile here.

Without breaking a breath, she raised her knee and got him in his adolescent jewels and down he went. Never again did that urchin bother your sister. To this day.

That trip through the Soo I was talking about earlier was another time I instructed your daughters to defend themselves inside a moving car, using only what they had in their hands. These days, it's those infernal cell phones. Anyway.

"When he reaches over, do this."

"Now practice. Slowly" I cautioned, as we were in a moving vehicle. "Practice the hand motion. And keep proximity in mind." Sure enough they both got the idea. I told them.

"Men want one thing. And you know what that is."

I do not want my children, especially my girls, victimized like my mother. Not do I want the girls to mistake con words for love. Too many missing women. Too many missing and murdered Indigenous women.

So I can only do what I can. I do tell my story given the audience.

Hang on to your traditions. Find your traditions. Find your language. Find your spirit. Find your place inside of yourself when all else fails. Hang on and fight to keep life in dignity. Be proud of who you are. Stand up. Fight back against injustice.

Reminds me of the time I was in Ryerson and this idiot professor who kept praising himself with the indigenous work, blurted something out, "Like a drunken Indian."

Well that did not go well. After class, I went up to him and asked him point blank if that is what he really said. I could see the pores on his nose and forehead drip with sweat.

The next class he came up to the front of the class and apologized profusely. Only after then did my classmates come up to me and pound my shoulders and congratulate me for speaking up. I remember when that event occurred. I looked around the class. I was sitting on the end row next to the wall, sort of to the front. All heads were trained on the teacher. No one looked at me. Did I imagine I heard this? Was it a miscue?

Turns out, they all heard it. But not one, and I repeat, not one fellow student contested or questioned or spoke up. In any way. The teaching. Be a warrior. Stand up for yourself, because no one else will. If you die, so what? You will go out in a good way.

By the way, son, I was the only Nish student. Smiles please.

11.

NNWE-BIN
(REST)

Like a firefly we come into life aglow. With this burst of flame we take our place in the circle. This hoop holds our place and responsibilities. All is sacred. All comes from the Creator. All is returned to the Creator. Each skill or power we have comes from the Creator. As all comes from the Creator, all must be held in its highest and deepest respect. This includes the mountains, rocks, sand, soil, trees, birds, and waters. The air and skies must be kept clean as our minds, bodies, and spirits. Each is also sacred. Each shall be protected. Each shall be thanked.

To know life is to know the sacred. To breathe life is to know and act on our individual and specific responsibility. This responsibility and honor comes from one's name. This is the name one is born with and given by the Creator.

"Use your name, I shall hear your prayers, for that is the name I know you," is the Creator's instruction.

My mistake was to not find, or give you, a name. Mine is Zhii-baa-aan-a-ka-wad. My failure was to overlook your identity—your name. It would have been as easy to give you one myself. The clan was easy enough. You were of the bear. And these are the medicine people. The healers. The herbalists, and much more. A genuine medicine man would have found the name in two seconds. Or less.

But I didn't, son. My fault.

Your name came at the end. Had I been responsible, your life might have provided a richer substance between us and the spirit.

As my parents and grandparents, we relied on the benevolent. The aid came from the spirits that made up our world. Lloyd was one of those few and able benevolent medicine gifted. He is also one of the most kind, generous, and humble medicine people I have been fortunate to know and trust. I feel bad you never got to meet him while you were here, son.

ᔕ

Hope is bullshit. Some made up vague means of control for the masses. I am not of the masses. I am one kernel of sand. One grain of sand.

One orbit in an infinite world of dark. I want my time to end now. I no longer want to be the strong one. I no longer wish to be the wise one. I no longer wish to wear the mantle of Pops, Grandpa, Uncle, Big brother, and whatever else. A fish bone refuses to dislodge itself from my trachea. Let the fish bone finish me off!

This is bad, is it not, Ngwis? So what.

Perhaps I am going the way of a friend who lost two young children. We shall call him Horse. He told me his story when I was in desperate search for someone who would understand and perhaps lend a hand to my demise.

"If it were not for my grandmother, I would have gone insane, or something worse" he shared.

"She told me to go into the bush and fast for four days and three nights."

I listened very carefully.

"She instructed me to go into the bush and fast and not to return until I was semi-prepared."

Had my head been on straight I would have done the same, son. But, there was no grandmother, or anyone of the spirit, to provide instruction. All my trusted elders have gone home. No one in Wiky is available to take their place.

I do not even know if I would have been able to make it out of my house and trek up the hill and set up a lodge to heal. I was totally depleted, disoriented, and listless without direction.

I should have left you to starve. Irresponsible. I missed the canoe on this one also. I should have taken you to the bush and left you in a fasting lodge at puberty. Four days and nights without food, water, fire, or human contact. Without a flashlight. And without a fire. Just you and your thoughts. Your only company? The spirits, bears, and other critters of the bush. They would not have bothered with you. If anything, they would have visited and maybe even delivered messages. Just for you. And you alone.

I would have constructed a small wiigwaam from saplings. I would have hung tobacco ties for the directions. Before that we would have smoked the sacred Pipe and left you alone, until the fourth day. I would have instructed you not to leave the circle, and to not be afraid of anything. I also would have instructed you to not drink the morning dew from the leaves, or not touch any berries that might be around.

I remember Lloyd's uncle fasted for ten days. Each time he tried to sneak a drink of water, his aunt or grandmother was there to shoo him back into his hut. They purposely placed his wiigwaam hut adjacent to the lake. Thirst is a powerful draw. This child grew up into one of the most powerful healers our people have ever seen. I never met him. His time was before mine. But Lloyd's mother relished in telling stories about his deeds. Well, not his, but the spirits'. I did have friend who travelled with him. This friend has since gone home. And that is all I will say about him.

I should not even be talking about these things. There are secret ceremonies and preparations one must perform first. That would be all we need. Someone to take it upon themselves and convince themselves they are prepared with the requisite skills, help, or ceremony."

"Nope. Leave it alone. You'll hurt yourself," is what I have said to individuals.

Other than this, who knows? Maybe you would have come out a gifted individual with supernatural powers, as they like to describe them. It's not supernatural. It's natural. It's a natural for the Nishinaabe. Under professional guidance.

So much potential. And I screwed it up. For that, I am sad and pissed off.

I'm still here, sonny. I do not know why. Maybe those visits from the elders and others have kept me intact. Sorta. I do recall one such visit at home.

I got a visit from Urban. And here is how it went.

I was in Wiky after the funeral. I was in a stupor. I was not good for anyone. A knock came from the front door.

"Biindegen," I answered.

It was late afternoon or something. I think I may have recently ate something. So I was feeling extra tired. I just wanted to sleep but could not, because that's all I had been doing. Either that or eating. Anyway, in walks Urban. Now, Urban is a big man. He towers over me. I was surprised to see him, as I could not recall the last time I saw him.

I know one time was when his dog chomped down on my hand and would not let go. Funny, eh? Funny to me. Now. Back then, not so funny. I was over at his store and thought to pat the mutt. He had other ideas. Chomp! And there we were. Locked in toothed embrace. Yet another funny thing, he did not draw blood or break skin. He knew just exactly the amount of pressure to apply on his canines.

"Go get Urban," I told whoever.

Meanwhile, the doggie was locked in full embrace. Urban could not have come out of his store quick enough. Without further ado, the dog released his hold. And all Urban had to do was tell it so. Nothing came from that meeting. I held no grudge. Nor he. As far as the mutt, I don't recall ever seeing him again.

It was this Urban that came and sat beside the couch. I did not bother getting up. I sat there like the lump.

"Maanda," he handed over a package of cigarettes.

I accepted.

In Odawa, he said, "A great event has befallen on you."

I probably nodded. I may have told him of your fatal snow-mobile accident. Urban is a man of few words. He did or may have said more, but if he did, I cannot recall. But, I do remember his paw on my hand. His bear-sized left hand rested on my right hand which was atop the couch end. That is what I remember. The love. The compassion. The warmth.

I do not remember any words. This is why I say, shut up!

Keep your mouth shut. The bereaved cannot retain the words. It's the action that matters the most. It's the hug. Not the handshake. Although that's welcome.

He stayed for a while. Not long. Just enough. While he sat there in quiet presence, he did not offer any platitudes or clichés. He was emotionally present. That's what mattered. Then he got up, and exited by the same door he entered.

To this day he asks how I might be doing. And he always sends a pack or two of smokes as gifts. For free. Without charge. This is Nishinaabe culture. Share freely. Give without expecting something in return.

No wonder we lost continents. We are too eager to share. And we end up paying the price.

In the case of Urban, I know I can call on him. I can call on Terry, 'Chi-Brian, Barb, Al, and more. Here is the source of that help.

The medicine wheel or hoop has another layer or wheel attached to it. This is the Dream Catcher. In the Dream Catcher is the caretaker, just as we are caretakers. The caretaker's job is to reap the benefits, sift through the catchings, take the good, and discard the remainder.

In the case of the sacred hoop, we are in, or at the center of the cosmos. This is the cosmology. The source of all things. And the final stop of all. The alpha and the omega. There is a beginning and there is an end. Yet, there is no beginning, just as the end does not exist.

Within this same sacred hoop is the Dream Catcher. Depending on one's take, and context, or circumstance, Esibikenh, is not only the symbol, but the actual physical entity assigned to manage the fruits of its creation – the web.

Thus the popular teaching of the Dream Catcher. Pop culture has missed its true purpose. More importantly, it has missed the sacred source of the web and its caretaker, and has assigned a commercial value over the purchaser's purpose in life. The dream catcher idea originated from its keepers, the Nishinaabe and other indigenous cousins, and it went trading post. It went from the sacred and a tool, and direction for life, to a cultural curiosity, with its only purpose as a sales item. Source of a quick buck.

The true and original spider webs and their people, humans, and their soldiers, the Esibikenh, remain in the periphery and away from attention. They are a lodge within the larger lodge of life – maadiziwin—which is what I call the sacred hoop.

The web within the hoop catches all. There is no escape. We are the feed for the Esibikenh. The general manager is Nanabozho. His assistants are the wolves, dogs, woodpeckers, eagles, ants, living and breathing in the air, waters, soils, and fires. Nimkii is one of the main caretakers. Nimkii's job is to keep the hoop clean of dark hearts.

Once in a while he burns those or things that have maxed out their purpose in maadiziwin, and move from one place to another. Truly a sad state if emotions are applied. Thus the fires.

The fire is at the center. Not only is it at the center, but it's within us. As human beings, when we expire and have reached our potential, our fire dies.

Gii-zhko-waas-i-geh is the way I have always heard it from my first recollections as a child on the farm. It was one of the most common terms I heard. His or her fire was extinguished. We never know when our fires will extinguish, thus the urgency to do something good that day. Our people commit acts of goodness when they hear someone has died. And this happened to us.

On arrival in Michigan, one of my friends offered to loan twenty-five hundred dollars. I thanked him for the offer, "Miigwetch, but I have no way of paying you back."

I knew I was broke and steady income was now in the toilet.

Other colleagues took up a collection. They asked for my needs. And I told them frankly, cash please. You know they took up two cash drives and came up with eight-hundred dollars or so. Again, I think it was Marty and his family who came up with some three-hundred and fifty dollars. The rest came from the community. Somewhere, I do have their cards detailing their contributions.

In the Soo, Garden River, and Wiky, it was family kindness that kept me going.

Gizhe-manido is the epitome of kindness. Gizhe-waad-i-zi-win is to step back. Built into that is to take or look kindly on others. Zhe-we-nim was a familiar term heard in the household. So off they went to offer beef, hand-churned butter, milk, carrots, and beans. It was the thing to do. One took care of the other. It was done out of kindness. And this is what we call our Creator. The one who is kind. One who shares. One who helps the needful.

Do we not need and appreciate kindness?

Thus the bedrock of singers and drummers and smudge people and general all around free help at your wake. The fire keepers and the wood for the fire and the shelter were all donations offered from the heart. The Chief of Cutler, Isadore Day, a strapping young and tall man brought a group of younger singers to deliver the travelling song as you were carted out to the hearse.

They followed behind the family, friends and other mourners as their voices helped to carry us through the heavy darkness.

Our songs remain the most piercing and haunting songs that touch the primal in any human being. The context of the song adds both pride and tradition. Sorrowful, we were, yet the honor and kindness that goes with the singing, I will not forget. The effort by the leader of the tribe and his group speaks honor, humility, respect, and support for the bereaved and for your travel home. That singing was heard between this world and in the next. Its ripple continues to resonate through the hearts and minds of those present.

Al and others kept bringing sandwiches, coffee, and bottled water. I may have got up once to fetch my own foods. But for the most part, I was served. Humbled and appreciative, I made sure to nod in thanksgiving.

The tribal administration community hall was made exclusive for our own needs. Employees were excused for the day. A day of mourning in our own space was unhindered. Nice, eh, son?

Every once in a while I noticed a fire keeper come in help himself to the food and drinks on the kitchen port. I did not have the strength to rise and strike up a conversation. To see them young boys going about their business brought a pride to your soul. And mine. I did not know any of them. But they were there before you arrived and were still there the next day when I followed the hearse out to the crematorium. For that I remain eternally grateful. A wake and funeral without a fire would have felt so unkind, cold, distant, and white.

Like an elder or one ill, I was chauffeured to and fro. Angie took care of that. You would have been so proud of her. Brian, her partner, was there with her on that day.

As I had left town with the clothes on my back, and my best top was a t-shirt, and possibly a faded shirt, Brian handed me the most beautiful shirt I had seen in a very long time. It was for me. It was the most exquisite, black, long sleeve shirt wrapped in a clear plastic case. Unique was the Nishinaabe design that dropped fully down to the bottom. There was a six inch wide pattern inlaid with geometric red, black and blues that announced, I am Nishinaabe. It was beautiful to wear on that final day.

To top it off, this farewell shirt draped perfectly and set the tone for the sorrow. Dark, yet with light, bright color.

No one asked for compensation. No one asked to be recognized. No one sought special treatment. No one made a scene.

Instead, a collection plate was placed at the head of the casket. A basket collected the humble money offerings. Uncle Ken seemed to be in charge of the cards.

When the time approached to close the casket, I collected the girls and held them with each arm. We faced the group. In a voice loud enough to hear, and with pronunciation, I attempted to extend appreciation to everyone. Those who came from afar and those from Serpent. So much kindness in such a short term had been extended. People offered their homes and beds. No one was left alone to fend for themselves. The hall stage itself had been converted into one mass bedroom covered with wall to wall air mattresses and camp beds. Children of all shapes and sizes ran free. Not one drop of alcohol was available.

Thankful for the generosity, hugs, and words of condolence, I called up my energy reserves. Like the staccato of the Papase, and the honk of the geese, and the orator of the robin, I attempted the final eulogy. Without a microphone, I again expressed my deepest appreciation to the outer-most walls of the lodge and the dead. I also wanted you to hear my words. No platitudes. Not once did I utter, "He is in a better place now," or, "He lived a full life," and other clichés. Clichés yet true, but surely one can come up with something personal and true to the individual.

Humor is key to the circle. Laugh at myself. Laugh at others. Laugh at life. During death, it's welcomed with another joke or funny reminiscent.

"Wake up, Priscilla," I said at my sister's eulogy only a few short years ago. I had been asked to say a few words there. Priscilla had nodded off in church. Not to lay blame, but that is the way it is. Everyone is sleep deprived. Yet, family and supporters continue. So when I saw Priscilla dozing with her chin resting on her chest, I asked her to stay awake. And that time with a microphone. With a start she sheepishly returned. Mind you, I had commanded that instruction with a smile on my face and voice.

"Did you ever embarrass me," she thumped me later.

We did not have a microphone in the tribal hall. Nor did we need one as the hall was cozy enough to not warrant one.

Platitudes I know you disliked, son. Just like Dad. Faked actions and theater we both disliked. Soapbox delivery was something avoided. Plus the hypocrisy of the orator made us both roll our eyes and want to throw up. People are so transparent.

It was all too surreal. This could not be happening. Our tears flowed.

It was as if our tears and moans kept beat with the ebb and flow of the great hoop. The chorus of hand drums and heart wrenching tremolo and baritone voices kept us together, in unison, and together as a family, one final time. This was not the family gathering envisioned. With great reluctance we marched toward the door: following.

Gimme a prayer. Gimme a prayer, son.

12.

BA-ZA-WIIN-KI-SHI-NAN
(Epilogue)

Woke up this morning to the dark. It was only 4:20 AM. Yesterday evening I had been outlining my story. What was I going to write that could lift the pain? What was I going to call my birch bark scroll? The points that I came up with only brought fatigue. I was determined to search for light and promise. What could I possibly reveal that I experienced in the last fifteen months since Shantu travelled home?

The results spoke for themselves. Most were dark, interlaced with the love and laughter with my boy. The grief, tears, and numbness fighting for anchorage would have to go and be replaced with life, good memories, and the crawl towards the simple act of breathing, rising and taking the hand of Nanabozho and all the good in creation. I was here for a mission. I was here to complete my mission. My mission was the writing of my experience. Perhaps, someone would be able to gain something tangible and applicable with their own struggle.

I remain not convinced. Would I have read about someone else's experience back when I was searching for help? I do not know. Not only was I too distraught, but I also was in great anger. I may not have wanted to do anything with anyone else's experience. More precisely, I did not want to relive the pain. Even now, I remain angry. Still unsure of the reason. But I remain taut and abrupt and very short.

Life, light, laughter, happiness remain distant. But they do appear. Flashes of brightness. I choose to go there. I know I cannot remain mired. Nor do I want to. But it takes, still, all the energy to stand, sit, and possibly chuckle. The act of speaking drains. The act of leaving my abode takes monumental effort. Maano, I think to myself. Let it be. Allow it.

Is it deceit and personal gain I scribe? Maybe. Possibly. I remain mindful to lean towards goodness. If any good comes of this experience, I do wish it to somehow bring a sliver of understanding

on the behaviors of Shantu and how he came to be molded. I do
know it's written for the twins and Shantu's brother and sisters.
If I leave a legacy, perhaps one day, one of them will pick up this
writing, and say, "yes, I now understand. Ni-sa-taan."

It was not easy, nor any easier to stay positive this early
morning.

I stepped out the front door and lit my offering. "Miigwetch
Shantu. Miigwetch NNMa-mi-ni-do-mak." Thank you my son,
and thank you my ancestors.

I heard the hiss, piss, ring, ping, pop, and all manner of fuzz
sounds between and in my ears. They tell me tinnitus is incurable.
Not only am I deafened, the never ending of a devil's symphony
attacks my concentration first thing this morning. This silent noise
never ceases. It goes on and on and on. Never lets up. Both ears
are affected. The cool morning was overcast. Grey to dark clouds
obscured the skies.

I watch my first puff of smoke rise towards a lone bird. It's a
seagull. If it's calling out, I am unable to hear. Undeterred, and determined to offer my thanksgiving for waking up today, I step off
the porch and stand barefoot on the gravel and green. Boy, that's
chilly. Even for a summer day. Dawn, has its chill. Dew is visible.
But I am alive. And I exhale a breath of welcome. The smoke joins
the grey overcast. I search for the sun. It's not up yet. If it is, it's
obscured by the kitchi-ki-zhep overcast. My hearing aids were not
inserted yet.

I scan my wooden and grey slat fence and beyond. No one
is awake yet. It seems. Immediately in front of me is my Impala.
Off to my left and north is a spruce tree taller than the phone and
hydro lines that pierce into its branches. No car has gone by. Most
people rise early. But today, it seems everyone is either gone or I
am early.

Welcome to a rez morning.

Underneath this spruce and facing full sun towards the south
and east is my plantation of kitchi-waabano-waashk, zii-ii-yiiw-
bak. No sign of my friends today, as someone decided to mow
my lawn and slit the young shoots into oblivion. Damn. Damn
for good neighbors. Previously I dug out a small hole from the
earth under this spruce and planted a couple of herbs Cousin Ed

had given me. I suppose it was his way to try and keep me active. Well, planting itself does not take long. It's the care that's a chore. The other plantings he had given me last summer are thriving in the back forty. Miigwetch Niitayis. The fir's neighbor is the aspen tree growing like a bad weed off to my south and also adjacent to the inside part of the fence. It also does not stir. It's too is quiet. Its leaves do not stir. I remind myself to trim the darn thing soon as its roots can reach and choke the water and sewer lines which are buried deep adjacent to its sucker roots. Hmm. My neighbor across the street seems to still be asleep.

The mosquitos and black flies are absent. They'll stir awake soon enough. Just when the temperature rises, they'll be there reminding everyone of their summer life. I remain barefoot on the dew. I am barefoot as I want Mother Earth to draw out the grief and anger kept from whenever and wherever. It's my own sweat lodge. A place of cleansing through sweat.

A sweat lodge is one of those purifying structures that one enters to sweat out indecision, and whatever toxins one may be afflicted with. Be it medical, psychological, emotional, spiritual. Since I do not have access to anyone with the requisite skill and experience, I rely on my own healing practices. Right at my front or back yard. So far so good.

When I am home, in my own yard, on my own land, I keep my feet free of cumbersome foot attire. I watch, I gather water, and I sit by the fire facing west and north alternatively, then shuffle to my son's grave. I may soak the blue spruce with a pail of genuine chlorinated Wiky rez water. I wait for rain. Wish it would rain. It's all too dry.

The spruce is a reflection. It's a reflection of me. When I reached home this July, I was shocked to see it dry. It seemed to be in in tatters. It seemed dead. The crown was gray and midway down it was reddish burnt. There was one tiny sprig of a branch that was a sick green. Its needles seemed alive. The overall scene was my spruce was teetering on demise. Unsure of the best course of revival, I studied my boy's crown. Yup! I saw the bandana as part of the problem. Even though the bandana was loose as I had left it, the swaying and in the wind left the tiny newborn tree with too much. The chaffing of the red cloth did not help. So I removed it.

Gently. Making sure to not injure or break off any of the brittle stunts. I placed the bandana gently at the tree's base, and held it down with one of the smooth stones from the wheel spoke.

I retrieved a pail of water from the outdoor water spout. I gave my boy a big drink.

"Come on, son. Get up off your feet. Arise. Live."

I also placed some semaa on the tree and on the four directions of the wheel. The rocks I had deposited were now a limestone white having been soaked in the winter snow and bleached in the sun. Some of the stones were askew and not in the exact alignment I had so methodically placed in their beds. I returned them to their proper place.

"Come on, son. Aabi-jii-baan," I repeated. "Bi-za-ga-wa-wiin-ki-zhi-nan."

It took some time to fathom or process this phenomenon. True. I supposed any sapling will or may not survive if its breathing is constricted by a foreign object. In my earnest desire and to hold on to my Shantu, I may have almost killed him, again. My selfish love and wanting him available for my own pettiness almost left me broken.

So it came to me. It was an epiphany. My tree was a reflection of my own condition. I was near death. I was not fully thriving. The very top crown of the sapling and the first three rows of branchlets were decayed. This imagery was telling me the condition of my own self. And I was a mess. And if I did not do something about it, I would die, just as that little bud was telling.

My head and heart were fighting to hang on—just like the tree.

"Oh my god," or something like that I thought. My boy is telling me something. If I did not dig or pull myself out from the depths, I was going to die.

That was the moment. That was the time, I realized deep inside somewhere, I have to get up and fight and thrive. I have others relying on me. Thus it began. Fully. Although, I thought I had been doing well or possibly, as best as I could, it was not enough. It was time to shift from low first gear to second low gear. Try to shift into high first gear. But keep going. Rise. Thrive. Live. And perhaps, the best or as good a lesson as the first, give thanks. Give thanks for everything. Everything seen and unseen.

This was the moment that nudged me towards myself. Give thanks for today, tomorrow and last evening. Yesterday served its purpose. There is no going back. Maybe today, just maybe, I can fully appreciate my family, friends, and many others who have supported me during after and before my son Shantu went home. And to act on appreciation. Miigwetch.

"Thanks, Dad," I heard.

ᔕ

The revelation is there. It's in my consciousness. I am trying to drill it into my unconscious. Life is in my head. It's in my belly. And I think it's in my heart. Hard to tell. For fifteen moons and counting I have felt barely anything life affirming. Eighteen moons later, I come closer to Shantu's birthday. November ninth.

This epiphany of self and my place in creation has become abundantly clear. Knowing it and acting on it another. On the bright side, it's a gift to know. The same time, the medicine wheel and my place in it leaves me struggling to get up and join the races. My energy level is severely compromised. Be that as it may I do appreciate what that little guy of a tree sapling and my boy holding it up from under the soil giving the inspiration to breathe, act, and keep walking towards the light of Epinigizhimowok. Anger needs to be discarded en route. And so will judging myself and others.

Of anger I at least am aware. I remain short. I remain impatient. This is my main issue. I do slip up with those around me. I remember telling my children hours after the news that if I do get angry at them, the anger is not meant for them, and they should not take it personally.

"It's me," I told them.

It is a daily struggle. I feel good in the mornings. Like today, I looked forward to my pressed coffee. I do enjoy the early morning silence and solitude. Gives me time to wake up, and think. Reminds me of other mornings when I hear music and assorted tunes in my head. My hearing aids remain on the nightstand beside my bed. And I refuse to put them on, until, someone is up. Only then, and for their benefit, and in my zeal to remain positive with communication, do I insert the darn things. The fridge hum adds to the frustration. It does not help. Oh well.

From the moment I wake, and even in my dreams, assorted tunes play in my head. At times it'll be the same song from two to three days ago.   Lately it's been Bob Marley's "Don't Worry, Be Happy." So I sing it. Or, "Every things gonna be alright." So I sing. Off key. Offbeat. Much to the chagrin and amusement of anyone within earshot. "Every lil thing's gonna be alright." Every lil things gonna be alright.

With my finances the way they are, I have placed my needs into the hands of Shantu. After all, he knows all. He knows best. He is with my maker. Whatever he or she looks like. So I know it's all okay and will be okay. If not, I am fully prepared to face the consequences. Losing my son cannot ever be eclipsed by the mundane.

I have seen the dark. I have gone there. Now, there can be only lightness. There should be. There has to be. If not, again, I place myself in my maker's hands. Do with me what you wish. I think and sense I will be around a long time. All it takes is one breath at a time. One step at a time. One foot out of bed at a time. One smile attempt at a time. One thanksgiving at a time. One prayer at a time.

It is now full daylight. I saw a flash of bright light off to the east. The thunder people have arrived. Did they announce their arrival? I did not hear. But I know they have made a passing. Holy water is now dropping from those clouds. I stand under the eaves trough and welcome the water splatter onto my bare feet.

"Miigwetch biish. Miigwetch Nimkii," I thank the thunder people and their gift of water. The yellow grasses will now take a hefty drink. So will my son. So will my prairie sage patch against the wood railings. I dug out the choking entrails of wild pea that seem to have choked my sage. When I first arrived home, I was shocked by the sage buried under the choke of wild pea vines. Now I am happy that my plants will get a drink of fresh, clear acid rain.

I grew up with clear spring water on the main road that Ol' Nawii that used to deliver to those living distant from this rich water. It was my job to haul water in pails for washing, cook-ing, and general household cleaning. I was the running water.

Gallons I would haul. Daily. And when it had run its course, it was my job to haul out back outdoors and onto the edge of the yard. Well, I had nothing to do with it, son. It's the way it is today. Only a few days ago, history repeated itself with my boy retrieving crystal clear water from the south end of the rez. Only twice have I seen these lagoons dry in the summer. This year the wells were alive and well with cold clean water. You could see the difference between tap and free flowing water. Life! Bottled water is unclean. And they have the nerve to call it crystal or spring water. These spring-fed cisterns remain ice cold year round.

"Glorified tap water," a cousin remarked.

Old Nawii used to deliver this elixir in a horse drawn wagon. All day he would parade back and forth on the gravel roads delivering this precious gift. Two fifty gallon barrels filled to the top, splashed over the top as his horses kept time. It was his life. It was a living. My people worked hard. They maintained a strong work ethic. They still do. Fluoride free water is still there for our ceremonies and replenishment. Miigwetch Manido.

But no one draws from the well anymore. Yet, the spring runs continuously. Civilization has reached us. No wonder we are so sick now. Nishinaabe have the highest mortality rate of any group. Diabetes, obesity, hyper-tension, and the ilk now provide careers for the health and social service agencies. Piped in water into every household has made us weak.

But, it's still water. We know we have more water than the rest of the world. For these people marooned with non-existent clean waters I speak and pray on their behalf. When I remember. I accept my lucky stars for my good fortune, being born in the geography my folks and ancestors call home. Miigwetch.

So I took a puff of semaa and blew it towards the sky. Miigwetch Nimkii. Miigwetch Nibi. Heaven knows we need water.

All systems go.

No one is awake yet. I'm getting hungry. But I do not want to start cooking breakfast, as I wish not to wake anyone. The smell of breakfast will wake them. And I certainly do not like to wake early. So out of love, I wait for stirrings. My diabetes can wait. To hold my sugar at bay, I ate my second banana. The first, when I got out of bed. Just as long as I get something into my tummy, I will be okay. As much as I dislike bacon and eggs, I crave it at times with equal cravings. Too much grease is unhealthy. Not good for my cholesterol or blood pressure. Darn. I do wish the household would stir and then I can get something substantial like good old processed toasted white bread. Yuck. The butter does make it tasty. Salted. Has to be salted. Not good. I get it. A lifetime of habits are difficult to change.

When I get hungry, exasperated by dwindling sugar and the food it comes from, my temper does arise. I constantly have to keep an eye on myself. I must be vigilant of my thoughts and the emotions that trigger them. I have told many times that I now am worse with my outbreaks. The words that spew forth from my mouth can be hurtful. So, I do have to keep myself in check. Meanwhile, the melancholy of my boy's departure remains constant. That in of itself is enough to want to withdraw, and if I try to say something to contribute to a discussion, there is the undercurrent of sadness, anger, and at times resignation. So I use up my precious reserves to not only exist but to hold myself in check. And this takes energy. And I have only so much in my tank. So I retreat. I hide in my room.

I keep withdrawn. I'm asocial. Since I have arrived home, I have been to one place to visit. I cannot carry a decent conversation. Nor do I have the patience to listen to what I consider banal. My bad, as they say. But I do try to smile and maybe, just maybe chuckle at someone's own humor. I think the first time I actually laughed was last summer when I visited Nick. That was a start, was it not?

I do chuckle and laugh a bit more often. I do enjoy those moments. Laughter is good. Laughter is healing as it is to cry. Being Nishnob, humor abounds at every opportunity. I try to stay with mouth open and cheeks pushed to the sides so I can smile. I do. Maybe not enough. But, it's where I am.

I should mention that Nick has lost his second son to death. Or was it his third? My god! I do not know if I could survive. I'd probably find the nearest and deepest lake. Or a cliff. Prayers for that man, my friend. I had the energy to talk to him only twice. Over the phone. I have not seen him in person. I am chicken. I feel I do not have the strength. Or I am selfish with my renewing strength. I am so involved in keeping myself alive, and hang on to those bright flashes that pop up intermittently. Perhaps, these bright events are permanently there, but I am conceivably unable to perceive them. But I do try.

Heal. Find a way to heal I tell myself. Make strong. Laugh again. Try. Try until success. Do not give up. Never give up. I have come to this revelation over time watching the hummingbird slurp nectar from the red juice in the feeder outside the kitchen window. I have come to this realization watching in awe at the sun rises over the tree tops. The green brings a lift. I have come to accept that I will rise with the help of the spirits and my son.

"Get up Dad," Shantu says.

"Nahaw, son. Miigwetch."

I will not give up. I will make my son proud. I will make my family proud. The twins, I act to please. It seems to be working.

I am told I look better. Apparently I have looked worse. Must be true. I do find myself with the occasional and fleeting laugh or chuckle. It's been a while. I have come from afar. For this, I feel good about myself. I have survived. I am surviving. Now, I want to thrive. In memory of my son. I wish to do great things with his memory. His infectious laugh and jokes and just all round aura of life I will share with humanity. Old and young. Any skin color. Any religious denomination. Any gender. I will throw into the universe my boy's inspiration, exploits, and spirit. I think his story should be told. The composition on my face will tell the story how I fare. For that moment.

There is my Shantu. He was part of the original Meawasige bike clan. Here he is with his daughters of their last summer together in Toronto. They are so happy. And then there is Shantu standing in the snow with handcrafted mukluks and mittens. He is all of four years old. He smiles into the camera. And there he is lounging by the computer watching the Calgary Flames, his favorite hockey team. He is wearing the team jersey. These are some of the photographs of Shantu that play in a slide show shown during his wake. Behind it was his favorite music.

In that show a description of each photograph describes the occasion. The one picture that remains with me is him with his daughters, Catherine and Chelsea. First there is a two-shot with each of the girls as they abandon themselves to carefree joy of being together. My boy is dressed in boots, wearing khaki drawers, under a black T-shirt. All are grinning from coast to coast. In the background is the CN Tower. The Toronto skyline.

"Little did we know this was our last summer together," Catherine or Chelsea said at the wake.

But before this are several pictures of him cradling two infants at the Sudbury hospital where they were born. And more pictures of him with the girls on the ski slopes. They look so cool in their outfits and ski glasses.

"Always the proud father," is the caption that stands with me. And he was. He was better than me.

He was a loving father. He was a giving son. He was a joy to his cousins, uncles, aunties, mom, and grandma. He was much loved. He is now gravely missed. He left an emptiness in his place. A bottomless pit of sorrow. That's okay. He was here to teach me something. For I am the father. And I have yet so much to learn from my boy. Heaven will tell if I ever will really learn. What that education looks like is a constant and daily chore. I embrace it. Not because I am so grand, but I must accept my life as it is now and go on. Not to forget. But to remember and pass on. Pass on what? I do not know. Fully.

Shannon or Shantu continues as a master instructor. He taught me about love and how it can be so healing and devastating at the same time. He has brought compassion. Be kind to those around you, Dad. Do not be so hard on others. Do not be hard on yourself. Love those who have lost their own. Speak for them. Assure them. Assure them their children have gone home and have regained the happiest rapture of their lives. Explain to them guilt is natural and not be too hard on themselves.

Yes, I too, have made mistakes. But there is no going back. There is only now. Tomorrow remains to be seen. Breathe for the second. That is, breathe for the inhale. Exhale. Inhale again, breathe out again, breathe in again, and breathe out again. Repeat soon after. It can be anywhere. In the park, in the car stuck in traffic, or in the board room. It can be in your room or in your bed, under the blanket.

Breathe especially when you are alone. Breathe in a crowd.

Anytime. I say this only because this is what I enforce and apply. Practice, and I mean practice, because it takes a conscious effort. Our body forgets to breathe. The body needs a jolt. And we alone Nanabozho. Each of us is the catalyst for life. We are the sole and only energizer. Lend a hand.

Everyone has a gift. This strength is reserved for someone or something someday. Each and every human being has this power. The power to heal. Now I have taken my power and use it for self-preservation. My gift for walking in the woods is natural. I walk solitary. Always have been. Day or night, winter or summer, I slog through snow, hail, and splash through rain and thunder storms in the night miles away from the towns and villages. I remember laughing at myself as millions of mosquitos sucked the blood out of me, one dismal night in the rain and storm way back behind Wiky in the bush. Or my pinkie finger almost dead with frostbite from ice fishing in the frozen tundra of Canada's north jigging for walleye. Forty below and four foot thick ice on a frozen lake feeds the adventure. Stubborn Indian. Laughter at one's self is the best medicine for recovery.

My gift is healing through discovery in the woods. The furthest. The deepest the better. And alone is the best. Baby steps back into my forays are the norm. Now. But I do take every opportunity to commune with creation. Be it in my back yard, which seems my shrine for the moment. As I gaze deep into the flames of my fire, or listen to the raven or crows, and watch the ants go about their business at my bare feet, I recall funny times.

One time my car did not start. It was a Sunday evening, and it was dusk. Craps! I was in one of the remotest parts of the rez. There would be no cars arriving. I was at a dead end. The road ended where I camped for the weekend. A huge black bear I saw the previous night ambled across a natural boulder bridge from its habitat on a little island just a quarter mile away from my spot. I had been frying bacon and such and deposited the residue off to one side near my orange canvas tent.

I was quite serene there. Through the weekend I had walked north following the shore. The shore was strewn with huge granite boulders and limestone sheets and smooth round pebbles of assorted sizes.

This was also the cedar spot where I discovered the largest dung pyramid I ever saw. Planted underneath a limestone cliff and overhang, I studied it with great scrutiny. Even though it was early mid-morning, the thickness of the cedar and the hundred foot escarpment added to the ambience. It was dark in that bush. But the reverent poop cone was clearly visible.

Stretching my neck upwards I was startled by a creature directly over my head. It was watching. I could see its eyes, ears, and brown fur of its head. Black lips outlined its mouth. It was crouched motionless. It did not move. Neither did I. Our eyes locked. He did not blink. I am pretty sure I did. He was taking in the whole action.

I knew it had to be his poop pile. Could have been Nanabozho for all I knew. He seemed quite concerned. The pyramid of poop had to be of his making. He must have stuck his rear end out from his enclave when he wanted to relieve himself and just let go. Over time, years, its pile began to pile. Thus the distinctive cone shape. The pyramid was his alter. His shrine for a job well done. Five feet high closer to the heavens.

Okay, I said to myself. The subdued light from the thick cedars added to the tension. Was he going to jump on me? Na. Just let the thing be. I won't bother you, if you do not bother me is the ancient axiom.

"Do not think anything of it," I relayed. "I'll be on my way."

He remained motionless. I don't think he cared. Maybe he did. But he kept his mouth shut. Tight. I on the other hand slowly turned around and headed for the sunlit shore of Lake Huron.

It was also on one of these treks that I came upon a prehistoric cousin. Except he was now fossilized. An elongated fossil of some four feet stretched out across a limestone slab on the same area of shoreline. I stopped in my tracks, bent over, then crouched, then keenly studied its magnificence. Whatever it once was now detailed on the rock. Its remaining bone structure shone in the sun. Which is how it caught my eye.

It had the long sleek neck of a dinosaur. Dino died here some time ago. Dino once sported a long sleek body and a tail as long as its neck if not longer. It was arched backwards. That is, its tail and head were stretched out and behind the spine and rib cage as if trying to reach the other. It had a proportionate elongated head, a nice rib cage, four legs and claws from its paws. It reminded me of an otter. Its teeth were pointed like any predator. Hmm, again.

I turned the slab over. The fossil disappeared. And I doubt anyone would be by this way and rediscover my ancient treasure. Archeologists and their ilk, would turn the place over and disturb an ancient burial ground and cousins. I did not want that. Unless one knows where to look across thousands of square acres or miles and miles of identical shoreline, the little brother is permanently hidden. Off I went towards my own poop pile.

The next day or evening I heard the crunch of large branches broken some thirty feet in the cedars. It was the bear. And it was following the shore. Not being stupid, he kept himself hidden as he walked by my camp. I did not see him or smell him. But I heard him loud and clear. He was minding his business. Brother bear was being cool.

Time to home. Click. Hmm. Turn the ignition. Click again. And yet again. The realization hit me. And I could tell the reason why. My indoor light had been on for some seventy hours because I left the door a hair ajar. All weekend. Dummy!

One thing to do and begin walking. I had work the next day. Could not stay here. And off I went. It quickly turned dark. I did not carry a flashlight. Nor would I have carried one even if I had one. I find I see better in the dark by the light of the stars or moon if they are available. Otherwise, I can still see. And the pot hole bush trail for pick-up trucks and adventurous four wheeled drivers was guide enough. There was one way in, and one way out. Ten to twelve miles maybe. So off I hoofed. Alone. It was now dark an hour into the walk. The occasional bat flew by attracted by the swarm of blackflies and mosquitos I attracted.

A pant of a large creature joined my stride. It was a dog. A large dog. Where he came from, I do not know. But we were out in the middle of deepest darkest bush. I knew there were no other campers or camps nearby.

"Aanii Nday," I greeted. "Aapiish naa gegii gaa-bi-ji-bay-yin?" I asked.

Doggie was a mottled color. I saw he was a brown or tan sorta spotted on white. And he was big boy. And he seemed to be quite happy walking in stride with me towards the first available house with a telephone. I had not broken stride as I was on a mission. Occasionally I looked down and saw he was a lean and well fed doggie. He was tall. Long legs and flappy brown ears. His tongue occasionally hung out and licked his snout. He did not bark or whine. I don't recall a collar on him. As if anyone put collars on their doggies on the rez. He was a free agent. And we walked strong and confident. Occasionally he would prance ahead and sniff the roses as it were, and join me when I reached his spot.

Maybe an hour later, I reached the crest of the limestone hill I was on and knew the first homes coming in from the brush would have a phone. I did not notice the doggie was gone. Until later. He was not at the house when I arrived. Explaining my situation, I dialed my sister and within twenty minutes or so, five vehicles arrived. One of them picked me up as I had begun walking back to the car. A quick boost and off I went. To this day, I thank those kind folk. Rez folk. People that knew of me. Or not. But they all showed up.

As for doggie, one person knew of him. "Onh . . . that was Ziitaagan."

Yeah, he went on, Ziitaagan disappeared one day. He was so and so's dog.

He was amazed that Ziitaagan had found me. And was still alive and in good health. "That was some years ago he disappeared," he added.

Many things happen in the woods. Creatures take care of me. I have shown the proper respect. I fear nothing in the woods. But I also wish to say miigwetch to "Salt" for that walk. Even though we did not know another, we got along great, and happy to have each other's company. I never saw him again. In hindsight, he was there to take care of me. Miigwetch "my dog." What were you doing out there that time?

The woods or open fields is where I breathe. Every walk is rich. Every step is invigorating. Each step is sustaining. Simultaneously, the earth sucks the poisons out of me. The poisons from diet, family and community relations, employment, world events, and the heebee - jeebee's of the spirits. Each bare foot into the snow is life affirming. Each fast has a purpose. These happenings have kept strong for the greatest challenge of my life. I now attempt to cleanse myself in the same manner with each foray into the saplings, shrubs, grasses, hardwoods and softwoods.

In my backyard with the fire swaying, I sit barefoot. My feet are firmly planted on the black loam, I paid dearly for delivery. Most times I gaze blindly into the flames. This is also my way for good mental health. Good emotional and spiritual serenity. The fire draws the pain and replaces it with introspection, action, and replenishment. Thoughts are of acceptance carried aloft by love. No, son, you are not to blame – not at all. It's life and the specks of wisdom that find its way into my memories.

Wisdom is gift learned and earned through the agony of sacrifice. Wisdom is a gift from the spirits – your people. It is a lesson for me for which I'm still deciphering and placing in its appropriate hub of the medicine wheel. The medicine wheel is not only a greater concept, but it's a tool and framework for life in all its complexities and links with the spirits and natural ebb of creation.

The Mayan and Egyptian pyramids are extensions of the medicine wheel. They are much more, but for the moment these ancient civilizations knew the mathematics and the engineering to express the practical functions of these remaining monuments. The Cahokia mounds of Illinois are the last Nishinaabe remains of a once proud and resilient culture. In Wiky we have our own. I happened to stumble upon one some years ago. Best if I keep this to myself, but it remains in plain sight.

The quadrants, and other compass points remain true to this day. Look at the Big Horn Montana site. These sites provide crucial links with the natural solar and seasonal beats of the earth and the sky. And our people knew how to live with this knowledge and apply it in an environmentally healthful manner over millennia. Dumb Indians, eh?

The spokes that emanate from the center reach out forward beyond and within and then back through to the other side, plane, level, or world. For the Western mind, as great as it is, is limited and restricts itself to the physical measurement. The center of Shannon's grave is marked with a tree with stones radiating outward and a "wheel" affect applied circling its circumference with more stones. Each stone is specific to its use. It's not there for ornamental purposes. Although, it is a craft exhibition if one takes the time to make sense of their and its overall purpose.

At the center is you, me, us, and all our collective relationship with the cosmos. Cosmology applications along with the cosmogony of its people's history, origins, and overall relationship with the "divine" and mundane humanity.

This humble and unassuming fir tree provides this story. But it also speaks to more. It speaks to the physical and spiritual bond with ourselves, others, and the world. It would take a reach for the Western trained or educated mind to fathom the total enormity of such a simple and seemingly crude expression. There were libraries at one time, but the Franciscans in the American southwest and the Recollet and Jesuit orders took it upon themselves to wipe them from existence soon after their arrival in Wiky and Great Lakes areas. What one cannot understand, one destroys is something recalled.

This humble grave in my back yard is treated with respect. The little fella of a tree that mark its center will thrive. As it blossoms, so will I. So far so good. New growth has returned.

I want my boy and tree to thrive as a unit. As a circle. Complete. One breath, followed by another. And the next. One cycle at a time.

For now, this is my job. My other responsibility is to help the young, our children. And I need my son's help with these responsibilities. It's a job I embrace. Shannon. Shantu. Papasc, stay with me, I plead at least twice a day. There is not a day I do not think of him. Until we join hands again I will do whatever I think, hear, feel, see to help others. If I can. Or when asked.

Shantu shows the way. Enough times he has returned to offer a hug, a smile, or words to help his family. Miigwetch, son. Do not give up is my continued cry. We need all the help we can get. I do. I certainly do.

I do wonder if we have a maker. If there is one, I ask my boy to intercede on our behalf. More than that, give thanks for life as it provides. I do know there is something more. There is some sort of architecture that brought us here and takes us back. Whatever. The experience I have is evidence enough. For me.

Let go. Let it go. Bury it. I snipped with the scissor. Then another. Finally the last. I cut my hair with one final snip just below the nape. With sadness yet determination, I respectfully placed the hair on a paper towel. I looked at the two foot long hair piece there on the paper wrapping. On the hair I placed a lid of prairie sage, semaa and cedar boughs. This was the hair that was once attached to my head. I had cut it purposely as my boy came to us and suggested that I bury myself. That is, bury my hair. The dead part of me. He came in a visit where I looked like him with our matching long hair. After some time, hours actually, I deciphered the visit to mean that I should shed my grief. So I did.

Only after the burial would my life renew.

I carefully wrapped the bundle in its homemade coffin. That done, I got up from my chair and walked outside to the fire. And into the fire it went. I watched until it was gone. The fire had taken my grief. But I was still sad. There was that something in me that was new. Not necessarily brand new, but something anew about starting over with growing my hair over from the beginning and beginning a new life. Not what I would have expected, but it was something I had to do. For me. And I suppose for those in my circle.

The gray, white and black hair was now gone. I had raised the bundle to the western doorway, and said something like, "Okay, here you go. Miigwetch"

With a look to the fir tree, medicine wheel, and burial ground, I saw the circle of life. Shannon's life was over. In this plane. And it continued rolling on the next. As will mine someday. I nodded in thanks, and return to the house.

This action was only three full moons after my son stepped through the western doorway. In the visit, my boy was me and I him. One of us had short hair. And it was me. Thus the snip of a scissor. And I did not want a salon job. I wanted to be true to custom and have my hair hacked. Without the aid of a mirror, I gave myself a haircut. And a hack job it was. I was told I missed some stands. To this day those longer strands I missed remain.

In the old days, this is how it was done. Back then, men and women sported fashionable hairstyles, braids, and wrappings and adornments. With death's arrival, it was time to do away with any strength and pride attributed to the locks and replace with humility, and more importantly, place the proper homage to the fragile link between life and death. And to show someone close has died.

This was my case. Death had paid a visit and crept home into each and every strand. It had to go. I loved my hair, not to the point of vanity, but for cultural identity, pride, and tradition. In a practical sense, the expense with barbers, stylists and such and the time for appointments got me away from a regular cutting. The heck with that. Besides my hair is the bristly hog type. It stands straight out and up like a porcupine's.

This decision must have been back when I was twenty something. When I was twenty something. Brush cuts were not conducive to my identity. I gave up trying to conform. Not that I was trying hard. Or putting a great deal of emphasis on it. It became quite clear in high school that I would never be white. So I quit trying to pass as one.

Besides, I resented the boarding and residential schools' legacies Canada and the United States ran for one-hundred and fifty years or so. The governments sanctioned it and came up with legislations, and the churches carried them out. All of them. From the Mennonite, to the United, to the Catholic, and to the Anglican. Their job was to save the man and kill the Indian. That was their mandate. And they were effective. This is the reason why we have dislodged children and children of dysfunction. The residential schools did not provide for good parenting. Only a parent can. But how can one be a good parent if an infant or child is seized from the home, under the threat of imprisonment, or fines, or death, at the hands of the Royal Canadian Mounted Police and assorted police agencies in the US?

In high school a teacher actually took a micrometer to further alienate and to prove his point about a superior race. He took a micrometer and measured the width of one of my hair strands against a white kid. Mine was twice the thickness. He did not stop there, he went on to show the complexion of my skin with another white student in auto shop class. We were told I was different and in so many words, that I would or could not ever be white. I did not ever recall ever wanting to be white. But this literal descendent of Columbus was again repeating history. Indians were less than human or at the very least, not white.

Reminds of the story when the US Army experimented with long-haired Indians and the brush cut type. The army wanted to see if there was any validity to the Indian's argument that hair was their power. Curious, or they had nothing better to do, they took two groups of Indians. One group with long hair. And the other with no hair. Each was put in a controlled training mission and observed their interactions with the "enemy." The brush cut troop were captured, caught or located sooner by the enemy. These warrior games proved that the long hairs were superior in their strategies and tactics. True story.

The hair is a radar. Its antennae. It is many things of power. It really has nothing to do with looking good. It's just that we were a good looking people and our hair added to the overall vision.

And another thing. Long ago a white man of some stature and social standing described the church and state modus operandi. He said, quite bluntly, that the first job, among other attacks, was to kill all the good looking people. We looked too good! We were a fearsome bunch. And that is where outright murder through biological agents like smallpox were so eagerly dispensed to unsuspecting tribes.

Some of us survived. I survived the auto shop teacher. I am handsome. But not tall. Strong boned and tough to beat. I see the made-in-America, (haha) physical and distinct features of the Nishinaabe in the mirror. These characteristics could not have come from elsewhere. I know a Nishnob when I see one in a refection or in others. They may not know it. But they are as clear as my family. They remain real Indians.

The shop teacher was not highlighting the difference in hair to build good relations. His job was to poison relations between human beings.

As for my hair after my cut, it grows richer, thicker but no darker. Darn. The hair is growing ever closer towards the waist. It shall recover to its full and original length and luster. Those few missed strands remain. I have not made any attempts to go to a salon. Nor are there any plans for such. My hair will stay as it wishes until my time to expire arrives.

Good morning, son. Take care of me and your brother and sisters and your mom. Take care of Grams and the rest of the family.

I stepped onto the cool grass. Barefoot. I placed the last of my semaa onto the ground and grounded myself simultaneously. The pebbles and stones and wet from yesterday's rain has kept the ground cool. The first exhale rose towards the hole in the clouds and up towards the blue beyond. Again it was early. Six-thirty. A seagull approached from the east and glided towards my stand. The front door behind my hair opens to the east.

I had stepped into the medicine wheel. My medicine wheel. My medicine. My medicine wheel was anywhere I happen to be at the time. I do not have to physically be inside my son's burial mound. As I stand with him next to the fir tree, less frequently now, I am now strong enough to not hurry over to his marker and ring of stone that make our spot and home. Twelve moons have come and gone. The twelfth was the most difficult. I went into super anxiety. The year marker was of much memory and longing. The change of seasons. I knew I had to relive it. And it was something I did not look forward to. I trembled. I heaved. I slept less. I was in terror. And with no place to hide. I could not run from my heart.

Others also remembered. They kept calling it an anniversary. What?! Are you nuts? It's not a celebration. It's a funeral all over again. "Stop it. Stop calling it an anniversary."

I have always associated that term with fiftieth wedding or x amount of years of marriage. I do not want to have anything to do with that word. Not in the context of burying my heart.

The twelfth moon came and went. April eighteenth came and went. I survived. Drug free. Booze free. That's survival. I want to thrive. In my head I know this, but my remaining heart and body and soul are having a difficult time catching up.

"What a friend we have in Jesus," the lyrics play in my head. Mary, mother of God, help me. Again it was early after my boy returned home when I was so hurting that I went to church, signed up as a member, and had an interview with Father Michael. At the next service I received the Eucharist. I think I went to service two more times after, and at least one more confession.

Through no wish of my own. I was baptized and signed on as official member of the Catholic Church when I was but an infant. I swear I had no hand in it. That was here on the rez. Wikwemikong.

I really cannot recall how I came to arrive at this junction last summer. I do remember late at night that a flash came into my head and quickly scoured Catholic churches and their times for confession. It was burned into my brain from an early age that I had to go to confession before Holy Communion. At about ten-thirty that night I turned my laptop on and searched. Sure enough, there were at least five in the vicinity. I think one or two of them had the confessional times. Phone numbers were attached. So I called one number. One church. No one answered. Left a detailed message. Hmm. Okay, try again. So I dialed the second. Father so and so, I actually have forgotten his name, answered. He seemed or sounded tired and maybe I just woke him up from his sleep. I apologized for the late hour. The third number also left space for recording.

The choir practiced and sang their hymns when the service began. Immediately that touched something inside. It brought relief? It also brought well-being. And I became emotional. I was alone in sea of white. I picked a spot towards the front, as I did not want to shake hands with anyone and exchange "peace be to you," with anyone. I was there for me. I was not there for strangers.

The magic moment in the service arrived. Time for communion and wine. Cripes. And I do not drink alcohol. But I did. Ever a so tiny amount. Just enough to wet my lips. Cripes again. I could tell it was real alcohol. Ever so gingerly I touched the challis to my mouth that the server must have thought I was relishing the moment. Not. The host or the body of Christ set off an internal reaction. If there was a Jesus Christ, I might have felt his entrance into my pain.

Satisfied I was still upright, I returned to my pew. It was then I discovered that the spot I had so carefully chosen close to the front was now a crowd of white faces. Darn. I knew I would have to be Mr. Nice Guy and shake their hands and wish them peace on our way out. It's not that I was disrespectful, I just wanted my solitude. I did not wish to mingle or exchange in meaningless chatter any more than required. So I accepted it. When the time came for exchanges I was rather pleased that their smiles and hands were sincere. But that is nothing new. I knew they had no idea of the history of their church over two thousand years. What with the crusades where millions died over Jesus and the genocides in the Americas.

I think a tear or two dropped. I know my eyes watered. I was moved by the Eucharist. Don't know about the blood from the chalice. I thought of you, son. Wiped my eyes as discreetly as I could, I kept my eyes closed and tried to not make eye contact with anyone. Not that anyone was trying to get my attention. I felt good. For a while, I felt spiritual? But it felt clean, pure, and right. So I was not to fight those fleeting moments of goodness.

On the way out from church, I went to Father Mike and gave him a hug. Wanting to keep it brief, I thanked him for his genuine words, of which I could not recall. The surprise was he knew my name. That was a jolt.

Sometime later, he bought me lunch at a nice place, exchanged histories and things of the spirit. He was a good man. And god-willing, we will meet again.

That was the brief burst with the church. I have not returned to service. Anywhere. The way I see it, my maker saw I needed immediate help and put the thought into my head. So I happened to stumble on a good human being who shared the similar insight into something people of a spiritual bent can only share among themselves.

I do tell others to seek spiritual help if I feel they have the query. I do not go out of my way to push one or the other. Find the one that works for you I encourage. This includes the synagogue, mosque, lodge, or any denomination. After all, the historical Jesus is quoted to have said "Love one another." With certainty, I cannot recall him giving orders to behead, maim, torture, and extinguish lives, or steal entire continents, or enslave its peoples in his name.

The two road wampum established the Indian—white relations soon after the first meetings at Plymouth Rock and Quebec. Each side agreed to "Live, and Let live," and not to impose their practices on the other. Nish America has never broken that treaty. Keep your way, stick to yourself and love another. Support another in times of need. And do be kind to one another. Not for personal glory. Or gain.

The angelic hymns from the choir reminded me of my niece's singing with her guitar and microphone at Shantu's wake. Lorraine, being a Christian, sang hymns all evening and late into the night. From the time they brought the body, and up to an hour or so before they closed the casket, Melanie sang with her heart. No one joined her. She asked for company, but came empty. Amazing Grace, which is probably the only hymn I know by name, and hundreds more kept us connected with the divine. Miigwetch, dear Melanie. It was so appreciated by Shantu and me. And I am sure by many others.

"I am so tired," she slumped onto the microphone a few times through the evening hoping someone would catch the drift. The way she said it was a direct reflection of her dad. She was being a clown all the while exhibiting the solemnity of the moment. We laughed. It was good to smile and emit a brief chuckle.

I missed that feeling of spirit and good. Sometime after the burial and everyone dispersed, I searched for similar songs on the internet. I found myself drawn to the spiritual music videos. One that stands out is Vince Gill and Carrie Underwood belting out "How Great Thou Art," but the one that brought tears was Mr. Gill again with Patti Loveless

At the George Jones funeral with their wonderful rendition of "Go Rest High on That Mountain." I wept. Not with pain leading, but with the pure soul of binding with death and heaven. The now and hereafter. Their awesome talent! I listened to this song over and over. I was trying to hold on to that peace that had been elusive all this time. It was also their talent. Unbelievable. What a talent. I wish I could sing like that. But it was Patti comforting Vince has fought back tears while playing guitar to "Go Rest High on That Mountain." Wow! I return to those videos once in a while. Alan Jackson at the same event looked so composed, but I knew he was not with "He Stopped Loving Her Today." There was not a dry eye in the house.

Perhaps I developed a kinship with George. I saw him in concert not too long before he went home. It was an awesome concert. Miigwetch, George. As I did with Willie Nelson. I could have shook his hand, but I chose not to, as I know I value my privacy. I did not wish to infringe on Los Lobos in concert in North Bay.

Awesome. I keep thinking of Richie Valens's mother and family when their son died in a plane crash.

I felt for Richie's parents. He was just a child when he went home. Or how about the parents of Janis Joplin, John Belushi, Jimi Hendrix, Jim Morrison. I especially feel for the parents of the boys and girls who fight and fought and returned home damaged, if they came home, from Vietnam, Iraq, Afghanistan, and many other places. Or the Pima Indian Ira Hayes who raised the flag at Iwo Jima. I weep inside now. Frequently when a community member dies. So many children dead. I try to say a word, maybe a prayer at times, for those left behind.

The ones left behind are the ones that need prayers. I try. Those who reached home are okay. They are in a place of peace and boundless joy.

This music about rest and escape to a place of peace and love and no pain kept me going in the most difficult time of my life. And I was looking for healing. I was looking for something to soothe my debilitation. The Holy Communion and the accompanying hymns, along with recent events have caused me to look at death and dying with a new awareness, respect and the realization, I, we, cannot control life. We are powerless in the sense we cannot delay deaths, reach or call back the dead. Each day is a gift, someone said. True. So I try. I try to value each day. I try to look on all as lovable human beings. Who of us can judge the other? Someone else said that, I think. True again.

Again, walk a mile in my moccasins is apropos. You do not want to walk in mine. Be thankful. And I certainly know, beyond the shadow of a doubt, I do not have any desire to walk in your shoes. Everyone has a story to tell. Yours is valid. It's yours. And it's just as valuable as the next one. Tell me yours. Tell me your story, are the words I have left with people across the years. I will learn from you. You have something to teach me. You are my teacher. Help me learn something new about life and myself. I will listen. I will not judge. I will not criticize. If need be, I will cry with you. This has been my message for years.

I now have another layer to tell. The one you just read. Much is missing. Maybe it's not enough. The fault is mine. I try. I tried. I will continue. Go with God. Go with your semaa. Go with the one that works for you. Even the ones who claim atheism. It matters not. The Nishinaabe view I walk has room for all. All stripes.

Son and Nanabozho provide the strength to go on with another day. They have given me their prayers. They heard. They listened. And they delivered. I know it is enough to keep me going and wake up and slip on my moccasins.

THE END

Visit www.KennPitawanakwat.com
Follow on www.facebook.com/kennauthor
Leave a review on www.goodreads.com

Miigwetch.

Made in the USA
Monee, IL
13 September 2021